THE CREVICE GARDEN

THE CREVICE GARDEN

How to make
the perfect home for plants
from rocky places

Kenton Seth & Paul Spriggs

filbert *press*

To home gardeners –
the unsung, cutting
edge of horticulture

First published in 2022 by Filbert Press
filbertpress.com

Text © 2022 Kenton Seth and Paul Spriggs
Illustrations by Kenton Seth
Photography credits appear on page 223
Design by Studio Noel

A catalogue record for this book is available from the British Library
ISBN: 978-1-7399039-0-9

10 9 8 7 6 5 4 3 2   22 23 24 25 26 27 28 29 30
Printed in Dubai

Front cover and opposite: In the garden of Shelia Patterson.
Back cover: *Townsendia hookeri*

CONTENTS

Foreword

This is a book with a mission, calling for a revolution in landscaping and seeking to enlighten the uninitiated and convert plant lovers everywhere to crevice gardening, which, in my opinion, is the highest discipline in horticulture.

A crevice is nature's first step in slowly changing the naked surface of our rocky planet into a piece of paradise. It is decorated with saxatile (rock-loving) flowers. It is a castle protecting and feeding these fragile plants; it is their home. Nature has also long converted ridges to flat land by the long process of erosion, but now it has the active help of people by means of agriculture, transportation, and housing. Crevice gardening has the opposite purpose: to give flat land some pleasant rock outcrops, made suitable to accommodate the pretty plants from mountains, steppes, and tundra.

In the name of artistic freedom there is a danger of chaos, a state with a lack of order, in a traditional garden though it may be perfectly interesting and colourful. But a crevice gardening has rules for placing stones, imitating layers of sedimentary rock, and this brings a feeling of natural order, balance, and harmony. The best crevice gardens, like fine Japanese gardens, reach the status of art that is not static but dynamic, with seasonal changes to their cushions, bun plants and dwarf shrubs.

For the past ten years, many serious lovers of natural gardens have been building their own crevices. This is because the crevice garden is a special structure where it is possible to grow hard-to-please plants, with its many sunny aspects, shelters, and optimal microclimates: there are many miracles offered by this modern gardening method. Both of this book's North American authors are talented and experienced in this field of knowledge. They are playing a 'New World Symphony' of alluring stones and sensational plants, just for you.

Zdeněk Zvolánek, Karlík, Czechia

Preface

Gardening was the final turn in the path of this solitary, curiosity-driven only child with a preoccupation for biology and nurturing living things. Dozens of childhood pets and houseplants segued into tearing up my parents' back yard for an experimental garden. Introverted and not fitting in, I developed an escapist lust for Europe (and rock gardening) while growing up in a small city in the dry American West. Later, backpacking enriched my amateur botany; working in a small botanical garden for ten years since my teens founded my horticultural knowledge; and an art degree solidified my work ethic and design. Travel landed me in Paul's garden when I was ripe to fall into a long-term love affair with crevice gardens. That careening path is now an unsurprising backstory for a nature-inspired garden designer, who, despite being only thirty-five, cannot imagine a different lifelong vocation than gardening.

Crevice gardening has been increasingly internationalized by the internet, but Paul and I saw that there remained a need to gather the history, provide a complete guide, and celebrate new developments and innovators – including more women – and make crevice gardens accessible to new people and urban places. Critically, they needed to be elevated for their ecological potential. Many folks over the years told us we must write this book, and inquiries from home gardeners and professionals alike reached a fever pitch as it went to our dear publisher, validating our endeavor to empower their creativity. This book is a tool for them.

I think we're alive at a time when humanity is experiencing an attitude change that nature is no longer a boundless place and inexhaustible resource. Gardening continues to be our most common connection to nature, and it may also be one of our best venues to act, to mend. Crevice gardens are part of that new mending.

Kenton J. Seth, Fruita, Colorado

In 1984, when I was 14, I went to the mountains for the first time. Little did I know that those early climbs in the coast ranges of British Columbia would eventually set the direction for a significant portion of my life. At that young age I had a lot of energy, and I was mostly interested in getting to the tops of these mountains, but what I didn't realize was that the plants that accompanied me on those journeys were seeping into my psyche. Fast forward ten years to 1994. I hadn't missed a summer in the mountains in that decade, and by now I had developed my career as a gardener. It was around this time that I was introduced to my first real rock garden. I was amazed by how I could instantly be transported to the lofty heights by the cast of characters in this spectacular garden. There, I was greeted by familiar faces from summer mountain trips like *Silene acaulis* and *Antennaria dioica*. At the time, I didn't really have much of a direction in horticulture, but on experiencing this aesthetic in a lowland garden, my emotions were stirred, and my mind was made up: I was going to be a rock gardener and I was never looking back. The combination of being a gardener and a mountain guy was the perfect recipe. That was 28 years ago, and my devotion to this art form has not wavered one bit. Finding mentors in the rock gardening community, and discovering that it has its own legitimate culture, I made it my mission to promote the style, which I have been doing now for at least 15 years. The publication of this book is part of that mission.

Paul Spriggs, Victoria, British Columbia

Acknowledgments

As settlers, Kenton and Paul respectfully acknowledge the Parianuche (Grand Ute) and Lkwungen (Esquimalt, and Songhees) peoples on whose ancestral territories we respectively reside. As gardeners, we share a deep connection to the land and would like to honour it's original protectors and stewards.

Little did we know when we embarked on this book what a project it would be. We have thirty-five collective years of designing and building crevice gardens and presumed we would pool our collective knowledge about this stuff into book form and a work of art would effortlessly appear. Nothing could have been further from the truth. It took four years and we heavily relied on the knowledge and skills of generous friends in the international rock gardening community. We could not have done it without their help.

In giving our thanks, we owe much gratitude to our mentor and teacher, Zdeněk Zvolánek, from whom we have learned the craft of building crevice gardens. Through us, his tireless vision will continue to disseminate.

We extend our gratitude for the patience and hard work of so many friends who volunteered to workshop, review and edit: Susan Sims, Rod Haenni, Lori Skulski, David and Wendy Sellars, Martin Hajman, Liz Knowles, Rob Staniland, John Stireman, Jeanine Smith, Jim Jermyn, Todd Boland, Marla Alexander, Sally Benson, Trina Lindsey and our *deus ex machina* Kristine Jepsen.

Thanks also go to Panayoti Kelaidis, Dr. Hans Roemer, Cliff Booker, Alan Furness, Paul Krystof, Vojtěch Holubec, Mike Kintgen, Josef Halda, Jîří Papoušek, Sandy Snyder, Stephanie Ferguson, Ian and Maggie Young, Julia Corden, Jenny Wainwright-Klein, Vladimir Stanek, Ger van den Beuken, Bob Nold, Adrian Young, Martin Sheader, Michael Mauser, and Dieter Zschummel. They have been our rock garden mentors and help to keep the flame burning bright within us.

A specific thanks to those who exposed their gardens as case studies, whose names appear where their gardens are featured.

Bobby Ward, Elizabeth Zander, Ty Danylchuk, Bryce Mcbride, Shane Johnson, Cameron Kidd, Chad Kreutzenstein, Darryl Clark, Chris Dixon, Jeff Wright, Janice Currie, John Sheridan, Diane Whitehead,

Campanula choruhensis

Maedythe Martin, Noah and Holly Spriggs, Jeremy Schmidt, Jay Ackerly, Carolyn Herriot, Jacob Mares, Peter Korn, Nick Courtens, Glenn Guenterberg, Patrice van Vleet, and Ryan Keating are peers and friends who have been indispensable company traveling alongside us. This also goes out to all friends and photo contributors whom we didn't have space to thank or whose support for the book was indirect – supporting us as humans – on this long journey.

Our gratitude also extends to the memories of the late Rex Murfitt, Joyce Carruthers, Malcolm McGregor, George Nation, and Steve Newall.

We acknowledge the great alpine plant societies, through which the majority of teaching is done in the rock garden world, and for us specifically the North American Rock Garden Society (from whom we received timely editorial support in the form of the Norman Singer Endowment Fund), the Scottish Rock Garden Society, the Alpine Garden Society, and the New Zealand Alpine Garden Society.

Thanks to Anna Mumford at Filbert Press and Michelle Noel at Studio Noel for turning our bits and pieces into the most beautiful book we could have ever hoped for.

Finally, we acknowledge our partners and most solid rocks, Bonnie McGrath and Tori Miner, for helping us endure the emotional roller coaster of writing this book. For this you deserve an extra-special thanks.

WHAT IS A CREVICE GARDEN?

Whether filling a patio pot or an acre of public park, the modern crevice garden is a style of rock gardening that employs the crevices between rocks to mimic the conditions that many difficult-to-grow plants need. These gardens are often built on a slope or as a raised mound or berm, and give the impression of a natural rocky outcrop. This sense of solidity requires that a classic crevice garden is constructed with buried rocks over at least half of its surface, versus the broad definition of a rock garden, which has no rule about how much rock is used. In the crevices between the rocks are planting areas which offer diverse microclimates ranging from cool, shaded cliffs to warm, sunbaked faces.

There is little open soil or mulch in the crevice garden – just rocks and plants.

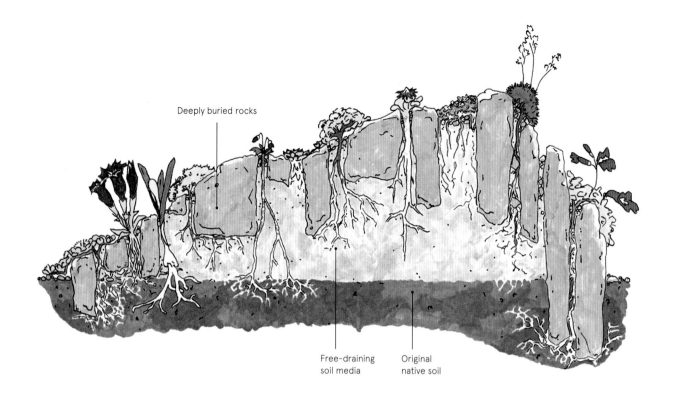

Deeply buried rocks

Free-draining soil media

Original native soil

A crevice garden grows plants better than other rock gardens mainly because of the way in which it channels and conserves water. First, the garden's raised form allows rapid drainage over sloping rocks. Secondly, the mound's more permeable soils encourage vertical drainage between the rocks. The surface, top-dressed with gravel or smaller rocks, ensures that the tops of plants stay warm and dry in the sun and wind, preventing the stagnant conditions these plants despise. Meanwhile, deep between the crevices and far from the surface, the plant roots enjoy more consistent soil moisture and temperature, safeguarding them from evaporation and fluctuating surface conditions. In a crevice garden's lean soil we can cultivate the plants that are native to the very edge of where life can exist.

Early pioneers of crevice gardening, inspired by seeing plants growing in apparently impossibly tight fissures in the wild, found that constructing a crevice garden at home was the key to successful cultivation of plants that had been truly impossible to grow before. Plant collectors have long known that some gems seem to require the conditions of a container or trough to succeed and alpine enthusiasts employ glass houses to keep their plants dry. These same plants are often perfectly at home in a crevice garden, which has the advantage of being adaptable in size and more natural.

Above: In the crevice garden, a wide range of plants can be offered a variety of positions for both their tops and roots. What happens out of view is at least half the magic of a crevice.
Opposite: Seed collector Vladimír Staněk grows a wide variety of plants in his sloping crevice garden.

ROCKY PLACES AND THEIR PLANTS

Rock-dominated places represent the extremes of where life can exist, for cold, drought, high winds, snow cover, short seasons, nutrient deficiencies, and even chemical toxicity throw a continual challenge at the living things striving to survive there, including human beings. There is a wild spirit in cultures that live in these extremes, and even when our species has ostensibly conquered discomfort, we are drawn away from our cities and safe suburbs (if only on weekends) to be death-defying mountaineers, oceanic boaters, cavers, and hikers. Once back on the edge, we are compelled not only by the colorful blooms of plants triumphing against these forces, but by the rugged adaptations of these saxatile plants (those that usually grow in association with rocks), where delicate organic life is set against its hard mineral home – perhaps an aesthetic metaphor for life on Earth.

Mountains are our principal influence and a huge source of inspiration to rock gardeners.

Penstemon rupicola. Observing plants in nature is the best way to gain insight into how to grow them.

18 'I am resolved; henceforth . . . so long as life is granted me by divine providence, every year to ascend several mountains . . . when the plants are in full growth, partly for knowledge of them, partly for noble exercise, and gladdening of the mind. How great indeed are the enjoyment and the delights of the spirit as it is affected by contemplating the wonder and vastness of the mountains and raising one's head as it were among the clouds.'

Conrad Gessner,
Historia Plantarum (compiled
1555–1565, published 1754)

Rock-dominated places such as this alpine area in Porta Vescova, Italian Dolomites, represent the extremes of where life can exist.

The underlying bones: geology

In nature, exposed rock is the result of hundreds of millions of years of plate tectonics heaving and shifting the earth's surface into dramatic exposures. Land is forced upward from below while gravity drives erosion from above. The geology of stone in any natural landscape may vary greatly, affecting the diversity of plant life growing there. Geologists organize Earth's bewildering array of rock compositions into three basic types: igneous (of fire), sedimentary (deposited sediments) and metamorphic (changed by heat and pressure).

Igneous rocks, such as granite, pumice, scoria, gabbro, and basalt, are composed of magma cooled inside the earth or on the surface as lava. These mixtures of molten magma, crystals, and gas bubbles are usually mineral rich, being composed mostly of silicon, quartz, and feldspar that weather into neutral or acidic soils. However, those that are particularly hard weather slowly and don't provide immediate nutrition to plants. Geological features made of igneous stone such as granite are imposing to behold, with their smooth slabs and spires, but are generally poor in floral diversity.

Top, above and below: Sedimentary or not, rock can be stratified and tilted by geological forces to provide inspiration for a classic crevice garden.

19

Sedimentary rocks are the product of the layered accumulation of eroded material (like clay, silt, and sand) and may even include organic detritus such as shells, corals, and other fossils. These are usually deposited in layers in an ancient river, lake, or ocean. These particles are then 'glued' together by either calcite or quartz under heat or pressure to form stone. Sandstone, siltstone, limestone, shale, mudrock, and conglomerates are all sedimentary. Because sedimentary rock is composed of fused grains, it can be slightly porous if they were not very compressed. Limestone is often softer and more easily weathered into soils whose rich and available nutrients host the most diverse natural plant communities. Not surprisingly, softer limestones have been historically favored for use in rock gardens for their porosity and high pH, which helps to supply water and nutrients to plants, especially in otherwise low-pH gardening conditions.

Metamorphic rock is any rock type that has undergone metamorphosis from its original state as a result of heat and pressure. Familiar examples include marble, which is basically cooked limestone and quartzite, which was formerly sandstone. Slate, gneiss, and schist are also common metamorphic rocks. Soils derived from them tend to be neutral to acidic.

Igneous landscapes are often dramatic but poor in floral diversity.

Above: Metamorphic rocks which have
been dramatically tilted after being
subjected to heat and pressure.
Right: Limestone areas often support
the richest floras in nature.

Saxifraga oppositifolia growing from a natural limestone crevice.

Habitats made of exposed limestone tend to have richer plant communities and be more interesting to the rock gardener.

Rocky soils

It's only fitting that rock gardeners should think of soil as what it is – busted rock. Soil is the result of the breakdown of the bedrock known as parent material, weathered by physical and chemical means into small particles that become a totally different material. Big rocks are broken into smaller rocks until we don't call them rocks anymore, becoming sand, silt, or clay. These natural soils, and their presence on Earth, are the product of plate tectonics and erosion. They are moved by wind and water, forever hounded by gravity, eventually going underwater or underground again to be reborn as stone. Coinciding with this stone cycle, the life and death of carbon-based organic material goes on. The living is birthed from the mineral non-living, then co-mingled and fused into a mobile and dynamic matrix, creating this strange mix, both inanimate and alive, that we call 'soil'. For most plants, soil is their rhizosphere, or the environment where their roots live.

The soils of natural rocky areas are low in nutrients and generally porous, because the parent material (stone) has had less time to break down into fine particles. There is little or no history in those places of plants creating and building organic material in the soil to trap and store nutrients. The harsh climate may also wash or blow away nutrients or provide only a very short growing season in which the local plants can produce their own organic matter from decaying roots, stems and leaves. What's worse, the plants are often very small and don't add much organic material to the soil by volume. In dry climates, scant moisture also reduces growth, and thus the total amount of organic content.

In these depauperate places, plants have adapted to rely more on mineral nutrients than organic humates, with the parent material exerting strong influence over what can grow there. These soils are usually scientifically classified as 'entisols', or undeveloped soils. Entisols feature exposed rocks and particles of smaller rocks down to a sand, silt, or clay. Being so fresh, these particles tend to be larger and allow more air and oxygen into the rhizosphere of plants that grow in them.

In addition, many plants from rocky places employ bacteriological and fungal relationships with their roots to find or produce what little they need. Alpine snow melt also creates an interesting phenomenon: nitrogen held up in the snowpack floods the plants just when they need a good feeding to come into growth.

Sometimes plants don't grow in soil at all. In mild or moist places, plants defined as lithophytes, or rock lovers, can grow on the surface of the rocks themselves, and in harsher climates, plants vying for the first seats on newly exposed stone must grow where their roots are safely hidden in fissures and crevices in the rock itself. These are chasmophytes. Both defy the need for true soil in their rhizosphere. Crevices form in the weak spots of rocks as a result of chemical and physical weathering, which can include everything from freeze-thaw cycles to prying plant roots. Sometimes a small amount of soil, dust, or organic material will build up in crevices, but often any scant organic matter comes from the plant's own decay.

In nature, the roots of saxatile plants must reach deeply because any soil volume is displaced by rocks and gravel, if indeed there is any soil at all.

Below: *Anarthophyllum desideratum* grows in rocky soils which are low in organic nutrients.
Next page: *Silene acaulis* enjoys less competition by growing in places that are the thresholds between real soil and mere cracks in rock.

The climate of crevices

Harsh, rocky places on Earth vary from alpine ridges to windswept sea coasts and sun-baked deserts. These fast-draining, nutrient-poor, excessively hot or cold, and often very dry and exposed environments provide a distinct habitat that leads to dwarfism in plants.

Right: An alpine environment: mountains have historically inspired rock gardening.
Below clockwise from top left: *Phlox diffusa, Potentilla nitida, Oxalis erythrorhiza*.

Arctic and alpine environments

Silene acaulis is a classic Arctic-alpine plant that grows across the Arctic and appears further south in the Colorado Rockies and Swiss Alps. Plants with wide distribution make more adaptable garden subjects.

Mountains have historically been primary inspirations for rock gardening, luring gardeners to find ways to grow alpine flora. The alpine zone is exposed and open with lean soils and a short growing season due to prolonged snow cover. It's often windy, generally cold, and high in elevation, preventing the growth of trees. Being above the treeline in the alpine zone is akin to visiting Arctic tundra, except that the Arctic's treeless landscape and short growing season are due to high latitude rather than high altitude. Their similarity can be confirmed in that some Arctic-alpine species, such as *Saxifraga oppositifolia, Kalmia procumbens*, and *Dryas octopetala,* grow in both environments. Another classic example is *Silene acaulis,* which grows in the most northerly latitudes, but creeps down to more southerly latitudes by going up in elevation and can commonly be found above the treeline in many of the Northern Hemisphere's mountain ranges.

In the mountains, heavy snow cover shortens the season of growth, flowering, and seed set. Plants remain warmer and drier under the snow than if they were exposed, but because they spend most of their lives detained or dormant, almost everything is slower-growing. In exchange, their seasonal biological activity is briefly and brightly lit by a close and unfiltered sun, intensifying their vitality.

The alpine zone has both sparsely vegetated rock fissures and rocky soil where virtually every inch is covered in miniaturized life. Geologically settled alpine meadow soils are often disturbed by animals such as pocket gophers, but protected in the rocks famous chasmophytes and saxatile alpine plants exist including many saxifrages, drabas, and androsaces. Woody plants that manage to get a foothold can only exist as *krummholtz*, a German term meaning 'crooked wood'. Having similar forms to the buns and carpets of their neighbors, trees are stunted and shorn by the wind, resulting in low, ground-hugging forms that can be highly sculptural.

Arctic and alpine regions are some of the most inhospitable habitats on Earth where only the toughest and most adaptable survive. We only have a short annual window to visit these special places and learn about their floras.

Steppes

The steppe biome occurs on most continents and is marked by the winter cold of mid-latitudes and low precipitation, as it is interior continental. Imagine the Mongolian grasslands, the Great Plains and Great Basin of North America, the pampas of South America, or the highlands of South Africa. Most steppes exist between bitter winters as low as -40°C (-40°F) and baking summers up to 40°C (104°F). The majority also see a great day-to-night temperature swing, and nearby mountains often determine the timing and amount of precipitation. Grasses dominate the landscape, swaying in the unimpeded dry wind as tall trees are denied a foothold. Some steppes have expanded by means of human activities such as logging and grazing, while others shrink as a result of desertification. The steppe is often found at the intersection of forest, desert, Mediterranean, and alpine biomes.

Given the multiple stresses on steppe vegetation, it's no surprise that bare spots on the landscape are where saxatile species cling, with an astonishing richness and endemism due to population isolation to specific mineral soils. Plants of rocky areas in the steppe benefit from these niches not only for lack of plant competition, but also because they are distanced from flammable shrubs and grasses.

Here, rain does not leach important minerals like calcium and magnesium, and the soils tend to be more alkaline. The steppes give our gardens long-domesticated plants such as tulips, and continue to lend fine genera such as *Astragalus, Acantholimon, Delosperma, Eriogonum*, and *Penstemon*.

Petunia patagonica is an evergreen dome that hugs the ground to avoid brutal local winds until it can deploy its quirky veined flowers. Plants of the South American steppe must also endure occasional ash from volcanoes.

Thymus roseus in the Bayan-Ölgii province of Mongolia. The steppe is a land of extremes.

Deserts

Sparsely occupied desert soils surround crevice-pocked sandstone, features typical of southern Utah near Navajo Mountain.

Every rocky place has a dominant factor to challenge its plants, and in a desert it's lack of water. The deserts that interest rock gardeners are those with measurable winter cold. Fully arid, they have either a lack of precipitation or are pressured by heat, which steals water away. This scarcity of moisture leads to the formation of mineral soils and vegetation that cannot cover the ground. Here, parent materials are powerful determinants of which plants grow in them, and crevices between rocks can offer stored water, fewer competing plants, and escape from grazers seeking precious water in plant tissues. Many desert plants are famously armed to defend themselves, as in the case of cacti, agave, and thorny shrubs.

While the desert seems the furthest place from the alpine landscape, both feature plants that are trying to avoid desiccation and extreme temperatures. Their defense includes hairiness, waxiness, and a shape that reduces surface area. In the desert, twiggy plants spread themselves out to acquire the ambient temperature and choose favorable timing for photosynthesis. Others mimic an alpine plant, hugging the ground to profit from its temperature; *Petrophytum caespitosum* shows up in limestone or sandstone crevices and grykes in both the alpine and desert environment. *Eriogonum ovalifolium* also,

remarkably, homes itself high above the treeline and low in the baking deserts of America. What is more, deserts perform an important role in isolating mountain ranges and peaks as 'sky islands', separating their flora and populations, often driving speciation between them.

Desert temperatures can also vary widely within a day's span, swinging more or less than 11°C (20°F). Many plants employ unusual timing for dormancy, growth, flowering, and even metabolization. Bulbs avoid summer heat by hiding invisibly in the cool earth. In gardens, we have to be cognizant of the strategy and timing for these plants in order to grow them in less extreme garden conditions. Some desert plants employ crassulacean acid metabolism (CAM), in which their stomata open at night to take in carbon dioxide to avoid risking daytime desiccation. These plants struggle when they don't have a day-to-night temperature change.

Petrophytum caespitosum grows in alpine terrain and deserts.

Echinocereus rigidissimus enjoys real estate entirely to itself by populating crevices in southern Arizona.

Phacelia howelliana represents its genus in the deserts of eastern Utah.

Mediterranean regions

A close inspection of this Cretan landscape in spring will reveal bulbs and drought-tolerant rock garden plants such as *Crocus sieberi* and *Aubretia deltoidea*.

The world's Mediterranean zones feature a two-season climate characterized by mild, rainy winters (November to February in the Northern Hemisphere) and very dry summers that typically receive almost no precipitation. This drought period may persist for six months or more, depending on latitude and elevation. Snow is infrequent, or entirely absent.

Unlike continental climates, where plants are dormant in winter, many Mediterranean plants are dormant in summer. Some retain their evergreen leaves during the drought period, while bulbs and herbaceous plants die back to survive. Mediterranean plants are usually adapted to growing green and lush during the autumn and winter, then often enjoying a long and floriferous spring before summer drought sets in.

Mediterranean regions also offer up a good selection of dwarf, drought-tolerant shrubs such as *Erinacea anthyllis* and *Moltkia petraea*. Although not all Mediterranean plants are winter-hardy in all climates, there are many that demonstrate surprising cold hardiness, inherited from historically colder epochs. These often adapt well to growing in spring and fall when winter is too cold.

The Balkan native, *Moltkia petraea,* is a classic Mediterranean rock garden plant.

Maritime environments

Where the land meets the sea, rock will be exposed in the form of either coastal bluffs and headlands or dunes and sandy beaches. The plants that exist there have adapted to coastal storms with strong winds that carry desiccating salts and blowing sand, which *Sedum spathulifolium* resists with its waxy surface.

As in the mountains, the solar intensity near the sea can be high when the sun reflects off the water. It's no accident that many dwarf and ground-hugging coastal plants resemble alpines or also grow in alpine regions. *Armeria maritima* and *Silene acaulis* are both classic examples of species that naturally occur on coastlines and in the alpine biome in the Northern Hemisphere. Such species, including *Dryas octopetala,* may also survive Arctic habitats.

Sedum spathulifolium. The maritime environment is tough on plants.

The glorious *Sedum oregonum* is another seaside-adapted succulent.

Humans will always be drawn to explore distant rocky places attracted by the wildness of the landscape and the chance of seeing new plants.

35

ROCKY PLACES AND THEIR PLANTS

Ruin/Urban

Easily forgotten among the world's rocky places are ruins, cracked sidewalks, stone walls and concrete pavements. These accidental gardens show us just how 'young' a site can be and yet host plants that prefer to grow there. For many of us, a dandelion (*Taraxacum officinale*) in a sidewalk was the first plant we saw growing in a crevice.

Disturbed soils can appear anywhere on Earth where tornadoes, landslides, volcanoes, rivers, gophers, or bulldozers expose mineral soil that has had no organic history. We often associate 'weeds' with these places, but nature has also historically filled this niche with disturbed-soil specialists like many species of *Penstemon* and *Scutellaria*. It's not surprising that such plants won't grow successfully or for long in compost-enriched garden soil, because they don't do so in nature. Further, there are groups of plants that specialize on lands which are effectively toxic to the prevailing natural vegetation, such as serpentine soils: by surviving a special stress, they have the place to themselves but as a result are often poor competitors out of their element.

New places to explore

While the flora of the European Alps is well understood and rock gardeners have been growing plants from that region for a long time, the remote nature of the more distant rocky places, dramatic and elusive, leaves an exciting front-line of exploration. Plants known to science but not to gardeners generously populate mountainous central Asia, Patagonia and South Africa. Species that are entirely new to science continue to trickle into cultivation. Humans will be drawn to explore these wild places not only for escape from the bustle of civilization, but also by the wildness of each natural landscape. What unites the temperate rocky places is a tough climate and rugged, often sloped, treeless ground. Exposed rock is the only shelter for plants challenged by drought, excess moisture, wind, hail, snow, high elevation, little nutrition, toxic soil, salt spray, animal grazing, and/or a short growing season. Plants not only adapt to these extremes using similar strategies, but thrive and specialize there.

Survival strategies

Saxatile plants employ many unique survival strategies to withstand scarcity of water, insufficient nutrients, unfavorable temperatures, and a shortened growing season. They are usually short, slow-growing, conservative in their use of resources, and more rugged than taller plants, for which the environment is too extreme. There is plenty of sun and ultraviolet light, so they have no need for big leaves. Small, fine-textured, waxy or hairy leaves moderate sun exposure and prevent desiccation. Many plants assume a low bun-like or cushion profile, minimizing surface area to deal with heat, cold, drought, wind, or salt spray. Saxatile plants from unrelated climates may use the same strategies in their parallel quests to retain moisture and temperature, such as the mounded shape of both an alpine bun and a desert cactus. Both are trying to borrow ground temperature.

Cold nights and warm days lend themselves to dew formation, and many plants take in this water through their leaves. Many plants also protect themselves from grazing animals, whether a tiny pika or a herd of cattle, with spine-tipped leaves, thorns, thick hair, itchy hairs, camouflage, or cages of dry stems. Some are toxic. The roots of rock-loving plants are often very deep and tough, as they are seeking moisture, nutrients, and stability that is deep under a stone or in a rock fissure; it is not unusual for a plant 10cm (4in) tall to have 1–2m (3–6ft) roots. Many deep-rooted plants also have some shallow roots to absorb water or nutrients from surface condensation or light rain. However, some saxatile plants, such as *Sedum* and *Sempervivum*, as well as some cacti, agave and *Phemeranthus* (*Talinum*), prefer to store water in their leaves to survive dry spells and only have shallow, fine roots. Some desert species even have root systems that are partially deciduous.

Saxatile plants are good at timing. They employ a variety of tactics to avoid hardship, including going dormant, visibly or imperceptibly, or by using CAM (crassulacean acid metabolism) photosynthesis. Some grow slowly and conservatively, setting down deep roots before producing much growth above ground, while others, such as *Scutellaria brittonii* and *Epilobium canum*, employ vigorous lateral rhizomes to survive a shifting talus slope or to find new crevices. Alpine plants also produce their own 'antifreeze', or solutes, often in the form of sugars. This ability is switched on and off at some expense to the plant, but is incredibly powerful: the leaf hardiness of *Silene acaulis* has been tested and measured at an astounding -196°C (-320°F). It can definitely survive where it is not protected by snow in winter.

The bright color and large flowers of many saxatile plants constitute a reproductive mechanism, as they need to attract pollinators over wide expanses in an often short window of time. Tiny seeds are more apt to be caught in tiny crevices, and in the garden these usually require some amount of cold stratification, or cold exposure, before they will germinate in order to appear at the beginning of the right season to get a start on life.

This page: *Eriogonum ovalifolium* var. *nivale*, below, a buckwheat from the mountainous American Northwest, braves sun and wind using the same strategy as *Escobaria sneedii* ssp. *leei*, left, the snowball cactus from the desert Southwest with its white insulation and tight domed shape.

There is a full array of adaptations by rock-loving plants. Recently, more and more complex relationships with mycorrhizae, soil bacteria, and other plants' roots are being discovered and measured. Naturalists often observe certain plants growing together in a habitat, perhaps benefiting one another with shared airspaces and root zones. Specifically adapted traits come at a price, however. Most plants that grow naturally on well-drained soils and surfaces are intolerant of prolonged wetness. They are also more vulnerable to pathogens of organic environments, and may be adversely affected by compost brought into a garden. In particular, they tend to be shade-intolerant, stretching for light (etiolation) when grown too hot, shaded, or in a cloudier climate. Many require a certain duration of warmth or coolness to harden-off and produce their winter 'antifreeze'.

Unusually green for its dry homeland, *Arenaria hookeri* var. *desertorum* survives with waxy leaves and a hard, flat profile.

Castilleja rupicola's bright flowers attract winged pollinators which airmail its pollen across barren expanses during a short growing season.

THE HISTORY OF CREVICE GARDENS

A garden entirely devoted to growing plants in crevices is a relatively new idea popularized by Czech rock gardeners in the mid-1980s, but its roots are deep in the history of rock gardening and perpetual efforts to find a better way to grow alpine plants. There is no known 'first' crevice garden, but there are early flashes of its inception in the late 1800s, wherever enthusiasts in Britain, southern Germany and present-day Austria had access to the plants of the European Alps. One of the earliest references to crevices appears in William Robinson's 1870 book *Alpine Flowers for English Gardens*. He and others discussed the virtues of crevices as a technique for growing difficult alpines in the garden or as a way of capitalizing on spaces in dry-stacked rock walls.

Vertical crevices provide homes for dwarf conifers and other treasures in the garden of crevice pioneer Josef Halda.

'The simplest basic rule ... in building a rock garden ... is to remember always that the rocks, whether large or small, whether outcropping or in bold and continuous arrangement, should look as if they have been there since the beginning of time, and have merely been uncovered by natural erosion of the soil.'

Will Ingwersen, 'Types and Styles of Rock Garden'
Gardening Illustrated, June 1952, pp. 160–1

The gardens at Průhonice Castle had a large influence on Czech rock gardening.

In the UK, rock gardens became a common sight after the publication of Reginald Farrer's *The English Rock Garden* in 1919. This highly influential work pushed rock gardening into mainstream British gardening circles, as the accessible European mountain ranges provided the majority of new plant material with which gardeners could experiment. Nurseries and botanical gardens embarked on collecting trips and returned home with bags of wild plants which were introduced into cultivation. In 1932, B. H. B. Symons-Jeune described natural rock placement in detail in his groundbreaking book *Natural Rock Gardening,* and the results may still be the most natural-looking designs yet. His constructions followed the rules of geology, allowing whichever angle of tilt was appropriate for the stone.

Continental Europeans were also interested, especially those living close to mountains. The first recorded rock garden within what is now Czechia (formerly the Czech Republic) was built in 1886 in the gardens of Průhonice Castle, just outside Prague, for Count Ernst Silva-Tarouca. Designated today as a UNESCO world heritage site, the gardens' rocky topography facilitated the building of the large and impressive rock garden, and its presence had an influence on the region's gardening culture. By the 1920s, it had spawned rock gardening as a legitimate subculture of flower gardening in parts of the Austro-Hungarian empire. In his book *The Gardener's Year*, published in 1929, famed Czech literary figure Karel Čapek wrote that a rock garden is the 'great pride of the gardener', defining it as an 'alpine garden', because it 'gives its owner the opportunity to perform hazardous mountaineering feats . . . make immense straddles, do knees bend, backward bend, forward bend, lying and standing positions, springs, and lunges in order to avoid crushing a cushion of Erysimum, or of flowering Aubretia.'

Czech rock gardens prospered because their plants did. The continental climate is a happy medium with its own subsets of moist highlands, near-steppe aridity in places, and chilly 'Czech Siberia' conditions in the south. These regional microclimates allowed experimentation with rock plants from all over the world, as well as those easily accessed from the neighboring Carpathian Mountains just to the east in Slovakia. In the 20th century, however, during the country's period within the Soviet Union, its citizens were forbidden to travel west without special permits, which limited explorations by keen Czech alpine gardeners. Nevertheless, the rock garden's ability to host many plants in a small area helped confined residents escape their economic realities. Many would also physically flee from the capital's summer heat and air pollution to the sanctity of nature in small weekend garden cottages, where some rock gardens remain today.

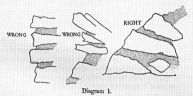

A page from Reginald Farrer's *The English Rock Garden* (1919).

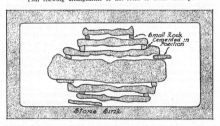

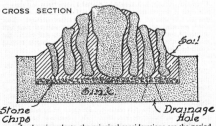

A page from the Alpine Garden Society Journal, Vol. 1 (1930).

Josef Halda is widely recognized as the father of the crevice garden.

Czech rock gardening became more official in 1971, when the Czech Rock Garden Society (Spolek Českých Skalničkářů) was formed. Travel restrictions loosened before the official end of the Soviet Union, and the Russian-speaking Czechs wasted no time travelling to the botanically rich and mountainous states farther east, including the Caucasus of Georgia and the '-stans'. Within their borders, the Altai, Pamir and Tien Shan ranges were just waiting to be explored. Americans sponsored memberships of Czechs to international clubs, seeds were more commonly traded between growers, and a golden era of Czech influence began as gardeners emerged from isolation and introduced a refined form of the 'crevice garden'.

Otakar Vydra was part of a group of Czechs experimenting with rock garden arrangement, motivated by their marked success with difficult plants. He first introduced their style to North America with a lecture at the Denver Alpines Conference in 1986, and in an article in the hardcover conference bulletin, titled 'In Czechoslovakia'. From this, he is credited with first coining the term 'crevice garden'. Since that early contact, Czechs such as Josef Halda, Zdeněk Zvolánek, and Vojtěch Holubec have toured North America and Europe, spreading this crevice gospel through writing and presentations and, perhaps most importantly, by constructing crevice gardens in both public and private gardens.

As a botanist, landscaper and garden writer, Halda spent the greater part of 15 years in the USA, building rock gardens and developing his crevice concept. His creations featured bold construction with boulders placed high, often tilted to a sharp angle of 45 degrees. Expanding on the style, Ota Vlasák along with Zdeněk Zvolánek and Vojtěch Holubec favored vertical or nearly vertical stone arrangement, the signature feature the public would come to recognize as a crevice garden. The collective efforts of these gentlemen determined that this vertical construction is the most versatile and useful for plant growth. Zvolánek, known affectionately as "ZZ" in rock garden circles, would go on to live part-time in Victoria, British Columbia, and write the first English-language book on the subject, *The Crevice Garden and its Plants* (2006).

39

In Czechoslovakia

by Otakar Vydra

Czechoslovakia is a small country in the heart of Europe where rock gardening is very popular. Some Czechoslovakian rock gardeners are members of AGS, ARGS, SRGC and other rock garden organizations of international consequence.

The climate of Czechoslovakia is generally mild with irregular rainfall and temperatures. Summers are sometimes dry and hot, sometimes cold and humid. Winters are often very mild with much rainfall and little snow, but sometimes very hard and long with severe frosts and temperatures falling to −30°C for several days. From the rock gardener's point of view this wide variety of climate, temperatures, and humidity is a source of much consternation.

Most Czechoslovakian rock gardens are at the lower elevations near their owners' homes, weekend houses or cottages. I am one of the few lucky rock gardeners who has a garden in the mountains. The altitude of my garden is about 800 meters. The first snow comes generally at the end of October or the beginning of November and lasts until late March or April. A good winter may have snow cover of 1–1.5 meters—very good for the plants and also for cross country or downhill skiing. A bad winter has rain, and sometimes the snow cover is only a few centimeters deep. In January 1985, after a mild December and a snow cover of only 5 cm, we had a period of severe, long-lasting frosts with temperatures descending to −30°C. The summer of 1983 had only a few cloudy days, and the climate in my garden seemed more Californian than Czechoslovakian. Under these variable climatic conditions we are obliged to grow our plants, keep them alive and try to help them adapt to the changes.

I grow all my plants outdoors without any protection. It is very difficult to keep a wide variety of plants from different climates and all parts of the world alive and healthy in a small rock garden (almost 50 m²) on a hillside facing south, fully exposed to the sun, rain, snow and wind. Yet, under these conditions many plants that are considered difficult grow and flower. I attribute these good results to a rock gardening method that seems to be more effective, offer more possibilities and give better results than the classical one.

The method is crevice rock gardening, and it consists mainly of placing the stones very close together. Between the stones there is only a small space to be filled with the proper soil mixture for the plant that is to grow there. Rockwork thus constructed also gives a more natural impression of an

Born in 1930, **Otakar Vydra** is a technician living in Prague. He has been interested in rock gardening since 1971 and has travelled in Sweden, the European Alps, Greece, Spain, the United States and the Pamir and Tian Shan Mountains of central Asia studying and collecting plants for his extensive garden near Prague. He successfully introduced *Potentilla ligosina* and *P. biflora* from the Soviet Union, and is an innovator in rock garden construction, helping to develop the naturalistic technique of crevice gardening. Among other special interests: baroque music.

Left: Article by Otakar Vydra in *Alpines 86*.
Below: Zdeněk Zvolánek, our mentor.

43

Above: Vojtěch Holubec helps to spread the crevice garden gospel.
Next page: Crevice gardens are springing up all over the world such as this one built under the direction of Zdeněk Zvolánek in the Bangsbo Botanic Garden, Frederikshavn, Denmark.

Crevice gardens have spread far and wide in response to interest globally.

Above: The crevice garden at RHS Wisley, England.
Below: Istanbul has its own crevices at the Nezahat Gökyiğit Botanical Garden.

Above: New Zealanders are getting into the game growing both introduced and their own native plants in crevice gardens like this one by Michael Midgley in Lake Tekapo.

The sharing of this style in an English publication helped to popularize the art in the British Isles, but from there its popularity has spread to central Europe, Russia, North America and New Zealand, where local gardeners found that the crevice garden style also allowed them to grow more of their own difficult native plants. The Czechs continue to set the gold standard, with influential examples to be found from search results on the internet; likewise, innovations from afield bounce back to the homeland. Today, major public gardens use crevice gardens to better grow and exhibit plants, including Edinburgh Botanic Gardens and the Royal Horticultural Society's garden at Wisley in the UK, Montreal Botanical Gardens, and Denver Botanic Gardens. The style has been featured in national gardening magazines, and even by American homemaking icon Martha Stewart.

The crevice garden's popularity is amplified by natural examples that inspire the style – the crests of the world's mountain ranges, the sea cliffs of the UK, and the rocky Mediterranean coast of southern Europe. In North America alone, natural crevices inspire from the Arctic, the rocky coasts of Nova Scotia, the limestone grykes of the Great Lakes, the fissured volcanics and layered sandstones of the desert Southwest, the dry steppe of the Great Basin and the sea-kissed Pacific coast, from ragged Baja to forest-cloaked British Columbia. Inspiration even emerges in the form of weeds that inhabit cracks in sidewalks and old walls in every city in the world. Made accessible by the boundless internet, crevice gardening's best is certainly yet to come.

The garden of Anna Milino on Vancouver Island, BC, Canada, enjoys the cooler summers and mild winters of a maritime climate combined with the crevice's ideal drainage.

Dramatic
landscapes
inspire the
adventurous
crevice gardener.

Inspiration also comes from roof tiles, rock walls and sidewalk cracks.

This page, top to bottom: *Sempervivum arachnoideum, Asplenium trichomanes*, and *Campanula portenschlagiana*.

HOW A CREVICE WORKS

Where plants grow in crevices or rocky places in nature, they enjoy better exposure to light and airflow. Rocky sites are often sloped or well drained, shedding precipitation very effectively and making them drier than flat places in the same climate. Water that is absorbed by the land surface will be displaced by the rocks themselves, forcing that water deeper. In a rocky place, the surface dries but the subsurface may be deeply moistened.

Slopes also have aspects: the cardinal directions they face. This creates variation in temperature, moisture and sun exposure, known as a microclimate. These are affected by any given aspect's relationship to the sun, wind, drainage regime, and sometimes snow cover during different seasons. The most familiar example in the Northern Hemisphere is that north slopes are cooler and south faces warmer, and vice versa in the Southern Hemisphere. Insulating snow cover, counter-intuitively, can make north aspects effectively warmer in winter than if they were bare and exposed to the elements. This variety of aspects, coupled with the variety of parent material, results in great diversity and endemism (species restricted to a specific place) among saxatile plants in nature.

Crevice gardens offer perfect drainage and diverse microclimates.

The crevice effect in gardens

Many of us have scratched our heads over a rock-gardening book that describes the ideal soil as 'moist, but well-drained'. This seems like a paradox, seeking the dual storage of water and air that good soil provides to plants. Most plants with leaves and roots seem to be tragically designed organisms with two halves wanting entirely different things: the top wants sun, wind, air, and warmth, while the bottom seeks darkness, moisture, coolness, nutrition, and aeration. Luckily, in the crevice garden, rocks separate leaves and roots, giving each part more of what it needs.

Above ground
Rocks change the way water, air, and temperatures behave. They direct water by reducing the actual amount of exposed and absorbent soil, sending some water that falls on them across their surface to their edges that meet soil. Less exposed soil means less absorption before the water moves on. Where moisture is absorbed, it is forced downward by the sheer displacement of soil by the rock, an effect that is doubly strong on a slope. In combination, slope and the impermeable surface of rock powerfully change where water goes. Water that is shed from one place will accumulate in another, whereas, if absorbed, it can be trapped and stored.

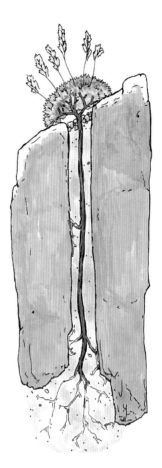

Plant tops and roots separated by a deep crevice in a garden.

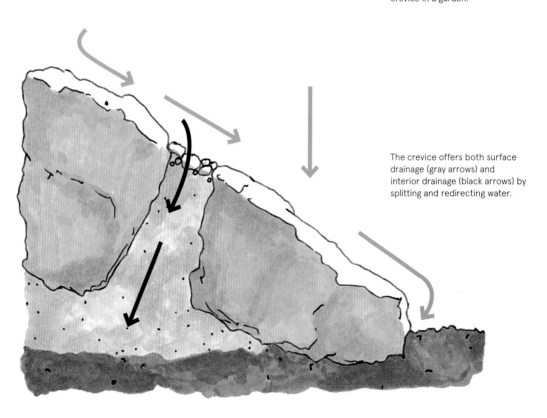

The crevice offers both surface drainage (gray arrows) and interior drainage (black arrows) by splitting and redirecting water.

A covering of stone and gravel, also called top-dressing, on a crevice garden ensures that less water is lost by evaporation, so the air just above the surface is drier than air above open soil (though this is less true with porous stones). Surface stones absorb ground and solar heat, speeding up the surface drying time after rain. A warm and dry surface also helps plant tissues ripen more quickly and better harden-off in preparation for winter cold. Rocks and top-dressing also ensure that new stems of these plants, which are susceptible to fungus and rot, are always protected from the moisture of the soil.

Dark-colored stones absorb more heat than light stones. Because all the stones in a crevice garden are partially buried in the soil, their color will affect the soil temperature and can be used to push a microclimate warmer or cooler. A warm rock surface in a cool climate will help plants finish their vegetative cycle, ripening and hardening their tissues for winter. Plant leaves generally don't burn against rocks, as it's only the very paper-thin surface that reaches scalding temperatures in a hot climate and this heat is dissipated by the rock and leaf's shadow.

Rocks release heat at night, and with clear skies, this infrared heat dissipates measurably faster. If there is humidity to meet this coolness by morning, water from the atmosphere can condense on exposed and buried rock surfaces. Porous stones such as limestone, sandstone, and tufa also release water, cooling their surfaces and the soil pinched between them by evaporative effect, allowing plants that want cooler conditions to survive in a hot climate.

Open-style crevices look like the spaces between the plates in a dish-drying rack. The rocks act as a more effective temperature conductor between the air and soil than a perfectly flat surface, just like the fins on a hot-water radiator. They also cast shadows on the soil and plants growing down in their nooks, as well as trapping and absorbing more surface water because they create a very textured surface.

Generally, the mass of stones in a crevice garden buffers roots and soil from diurnal and seasonal temperature changes. It also strongly influences water or sun exposure in seasonal ways. Sometimes what we observe in the garden evades our understanding because the physical interplay of water and temperature around rocks can be so complex: why did this plant survive, defying expectations, and why did that plant die?

Dark colored stones can offer a nice visual contrast to the buns, carpets, and cushions as well as warming the surface. In the foreground is *Arenaria lithops*.

56

Below ground

Welcome to the rhizosphere, where roots live. Rock garden chasmophytes, or 'abyss-plants' from the Greek, often don't know what to do with too much soil. Such plants have evolved to grow in even the tightest of fissures, where water is drawn more deeply into the rock through capillary action.

In open soils, ground moisture is drawn upwards like a wick if the surface dries, because of soil capillarity. A soil merely covered in gravel will insulate the soil below from moisture-robbing air and warmth above. In a crevice garden, the soil surface is completely covered with larger stones, so even less soil surface area is exposed to evaporation, which promotes a steady downward trajectory for water towards the cool and moist soil below. In hot climates, this reduces the need for irrigation, helping to maintain a consistent water reserve below. If the rock is limestone or sandstone, which have density and capillarity stronger than the soil, a small amount of water is drawn through tiny pores into the stone. This may be one reason why we find roots fanned out against the surface of these stones.

Furthermore, in some conditions where soils minutely expand and contract with moisture and temperature, paper-thin fissures can form between the buried rock and soil, which can act as direct pathways for air and moisture. This contact zone creates another phenomenon to attract roots: if the stone is colder than the humid air in the soil, water will condense and gather on the buried stone surface.

Right: The crevice below ground with roots fanned against buried rock.

Opposite: Ryan Keating's open-style crevices have strong benefits in Steamboat Springs, Colorado.

Light, open soils

While the rocks and top-dressing encourage dryness on the surface, a light, open soil in the crevice garden will buffer against saturation. Roots breathe air underground just as leaves breathe above ground, and they will drown if the soil remains soggy for too long. An uninterrupted downward movement of water draws air in behind it, bringing more oxygen down into the rhizosphere. The soil must retain some moisture for the plant's use, but the quicker the medium drains, the longer the period of aeration, allowing plants to breathe properly. A loose soil also resists compaction, preserving its larger air spaces in the long term.

Unless the stones are very large and deeply buried, the plants will eventually bypass the actual crevice as they grow downward and have access to open soil below. The depth of crevices in our gardens is limited by the capability of human hands moving the rocks; most saxatile plants that are only inches tall would grow roots several feet deep in a thin crevice if you could set rocks of that size.

In gardens and in nature, roots do indeed reduce the moisture of the soil as they use it. Then, the phenomenon of capillarity causes the water to oppose gravity and move upward toward the roots from below. In gardens, the soil below the rocks may supply moisture to soil within a crevice.

Aspects

We can achieve a lot by working with the microclimates within any given climate. For example, in the Northern Hemisphere, the north side of a building is the cool, shady side; the south side is the hot, sunny side; the east-facing walls will receive cool morning sun; and the west will enjoy the warm evening sun. The same applies to a rock garden. An outcrop is essentially a mini-mountain, with microclimates that are affected by the cardinal directions they face. A steep stone on an east–west axis can provide a nice shady shelter from the midday sun, while a plant that wants to bake will be happier on the other (south) side of that rock.

Making an aspect-borne microclimate is like creating a tiny foreign country in your garden, pushing growing conditions closer to a plant's homeland than your local climate typically provides. You might use the high and dry south-facing aspect for cacti like *Escobaria*, and the low, cool, and moist north aspect for alpines such as *Gentiana*. Eastern faces favor cool-blooded plants, such as most alpines, which vegetate in cool times, and warm faces favor warm-season plants, for example salvias or delospermas, which often wait until summer to put on growth and flowers.

Counterintuitively, less hardy plants can benefit from being planted on a northern slope because it will cool sooner in autumn, encouraging them to harden-off more quickly in preparation for winter. Also consider that a very steep south face, which will receive the low winter sun head-on, will actually receive reduced summer midday sun. An eastern exposure protects plants from brutal afternoon summer sun, and in snowy climates the shadow cast to the north side of a house can create the conditions needed for a protective snow cover, which may create remarkably strong overwintering conditions for alpines and even tender succulents. A good north position can accommodate plants that might have otherwise needed additional moisture or conifer boughs laid over them as insulation. The variation is so strong that the sunniest to the shadiest microclimates of a crevice garden often differ in surface temperature by 11°C (20°F), or two USDA plant-hardiness zones. Since rock garden plants tend to be small and ground-hugging, that difference in surface temperature is all they need to thrive.

Consistent shadows starkly reveal cooler microclimates within the garden.

Taking advantage of microclimates allows
us to grow a wide variety of plants as shown
here in the garden of Hana Ziková.

Thin slabs of equal dimension lend a unique
craggy look to this artistic crevice garden.

It's not nature, though

To grow plants from an exotic place, we can approximate the effect of where they are from and compensate for things we can't change. The experimental gardener will research the plants' homeland, irrigate, choose an aspect, provide cover in winter and modify soils to try to create optimal growing conditions. In the end, plants are remarkably adaptable and will meet us halfway.

Crevice gardens can even work for plants that don't naturally grow in crevices, but require dryness or drainage. Likewise, there are some shallow-rooted or succulent plants, even saxatile plants, that do not grow any better in a crevice. Others are simply wildly adaptable, taking well to rich, composted garden soils despite originating among rocks in nature.

The modern crevice garden explores the extremes of compromise between pure soil and pure rock. How tightly can we pack rocks together and still call it gardening? Can we still weed a paper-thin crack? This wonderful madness pushes the edge of what is a plantable space, and inspires us to test the boundaries of what we call soil.

Helichrysum milfordiae (pictured here in nature) is adaptable to garden culture in the right climates.

Some alpines, such as the pink dianthus below, are tolerant of a wide range of conditions, equally happy in a crevice or open ground and in a variety of soil types.

Advantages of the crevice

Two key advantages of crevice gardens are more plants and less watering.

Crevice gardens are the best way to cultivate the widest range of saxatile plants, providing drainage for wet climates and deep root-runs for dry climates. These gardens take some effort to build, but properly designed, they pay off with less and lighter maintenance. The multi-dimensional nature of a crevice garden also offers bounty, doubling or tripling the plantable space. For example, a circular garden on flat ground allows only 1sq m (11sq ft) of planting space. A hemisphere raised out of that same footprint has double the area. Adding texture to the hemisphere could triple the surface area, in the way that a sheet too large for a bed is wrinkled and rippled. The raised surface also brings small plants closer to the viewer.

Each part of the garden, especially if built to maximize its microclimates, can accommodate plants with differing needs just a short distance from one another. You can even use pockets of specific soil mixes to accommodate specific plants in each space, recreating conditions from the far reaches of Earth and successfully inviting an engaging international cast of rare and gorgeous plants to grow in their respective nooks. The welcome mat doesn't just extend to plants – wildlife species that need a drier niche, a clear vantage point, or a warm surface to bask on are attracted to a rocky outcrop. Crevice gardens also provide a tool for study and conservation by universities, scientific institutions, and botanical gardens. The ability to grow edaphic endemics – plants that are restricted to one place and one soil type in nature – may prove critical for *ex-situ* conservation of these species, replenishment of wild populations, or preservation of species in the event of extinction in the wild.

Two factors drive scarcity of water for gardening at the moment: population increases in already dry areas (such as the interior of western US) and increasing dryness and heat in those areas due to climate change. Crevice gardens offer another design option in dry zones and will continue to shine as an alternative to raised beds and retaining walls, serving the same function while also offering plantable spaces. Charismatic plants come and go with the seasons and their own short lives, but rocks remain for generations. In the crevice garden, we can see the pairing symbolize the story of life on Earth.

PLANNING A CREVICE GARDEN

Your garden's design is a story that will tell visitors who you are and what you enjoy. It may reveal a history of an obsession with *Daphne*, giving way to a tryst with *Lewisia*, or a mound inspired by a mountain range you fell in love with on a holiday. Maybe you just climb around your garden and admire the mats and cushions, coffee in hand, pulling weeds and reminiscing about the long, rich history of your plant collecting and cultivation. The fact is, most people are attracted to crevice gardens for two reasons: because they are the best way to grow a variety of difficult plants in a small space and because they just look good; a crevice garden brings the plants closer to the viewer like gems in a jewelry case, away from the competition of border plants and large shrubs.

The rock alone in a crevice garden says a lot about the individuality of its creator.

Historically, rock gardens have been inspired by nature. One of the finest compliments a crevice gardener can receive comes when the viewer believes an outcrop is natural, not built. Honor that spirit, but follow the logic of the site and be consistent with your garden's style. Your garden will have an incredible impact when it's inspired by your immediate natural environment. It may be as simple as featuring a native plant, as subtle as using local rock, or as nuanced as repeating local lines, textures, colors, or motifs.

A carefully situated crevice garden creates microclimates – warmer or cooler, wetter or drier, sunnier or shadier. You can warm it up by facing it steeply south or cool it by hiding it in a building's shadow, increasing your palette of growable plants. A crevice garden can shed water, catch it, or both. Figure out what your ideal plants want that your local climate does not provide, then site and design the garden accordingly. Also bear in mind what will happen to your crevice garden during the different seasons in a given location – for example, moist places may see moss develop on the stones unless they are constantly cleaned. Some gardeners in rainy areas use glass or plastic panels to prevent moisture on a section of garden at certain times of the year, allowing them to grow plants that, before crevice gardening, seemed impossible.

64

'If ever there was a place where rules were made to be broken, it is in the garden.'

Beverley Nichols,
Garden Open Today (1963)

Right: Crevice gardens can create microclimates, exemplified by lingering snow on the north side of this garden in the Northern Hemisphere.

Below: Here a suite of greens, in cushions and conifers, shine in their Pacific Northwest home.

Above: The APEX crevice garden in Arvada, Colorado, is crammed into a sports complex and surrounded by chain-link fences and tall light posts, but the longer view reveals the spires of churches and, beyond, the Front Range Mountains. By design, these nearby vertical elements are echoed by upright junipers, and the mountains on the horizon are pulled in by the jagged profiles of the outcrops. This helps to make the crevice garden look at home.

Container crevice gardens offer fascinating mobile galleries of a single plant genus: *Arenaria*, top, and *Sempervivum*, above.

Chris Dixon's tiny crevice planters demonstrate world-class artistry in small pans.

Go Small

Trina Lindsey's crevice garden fits into the awkward and small unused space next to a patio where small plants can now be closely observed.

If building a mountain range in your backyard is daunting, start with a smaller garden in a container, or a 'trough', as they are known in the rock garden world – a permanent, weatherproof container. Alternatively, you could try building a pocket crevice garden in an awkward corner, or even just a tiny one within an existing rock garden. Technically, just two stones with a plant in the middle is a crevice garden! Fewer and smaller stones are much easier to practice with and to rearrange. It's a manageable way to try out the concept and grow the rarities you couldn't contemplate before.

Regardless of a garden's size, variety and unity should always be in balance. Often, using the same kind of stone throughout the garden is a sufficiently powerful thread to weave it together. You might also repeat an angle, planting, or shape. Ambitious gardeners may even pit opposing forces against one another, like cool and warm colors, or soft plants and jagged rocks to create the glorious tension at the heart of a love affair with rock plants. The truth is, no matter how much planning you do, you will change your mind, so leave your options open. Experiment with new things as you go. A crevice garden, despite its hard stone, is a dynamic and evolving space – remember, a real garden is never finished.

Right, top to bottom: Repeat planting unites the garden; siting the crevice garden in a sunny and open, airy location is best; a crevice tucked up against a potting shed, where visually similar but botanically different plants unify the garden.

Below: A mini-crevice in a small space adjacent to a front entryway offers closer viewing.

A unity of rock type ties a garden and trough together.

Recurring angles give a cohesive
and highly naturalistic effect.

68   Siting the crevice garden

A smooth, flowing return to ground looks natural, like the garden is a protruding piece of bedrock.

How your garden fits into its surroundings will be one of your most important design considerations. Will it be in a pot, encircled by a path, a hidden feature in the back of a large garden, or an exhibit flanking the front entrance of your house? Sometimes a space calls out for a crevice garden, such as a slope that would otherwise require a retaining wall. A sloping crevice garden can gracefully manage a grade change with steep vertical crevices built right in. If you are considering building a raised bed and putting a crevice garden inside it, you could instead let the crevice garden be the bed, with its own walls creating the elevation you need.

In all good landscape design, lines of sight direct the eye to a focal point. Most gardeners place a crevice garden adjacent to paths or in places where they spend a lot of time so they can easily admire and maintain their floral jewel box. Always consider: what is the first view of the garden upon approaching it? Are there elements in the background to hide, or to blend with? The element of surprise is also a common theme in landscape design. Some of the earliest rock gardening books suggested that the garden should not be visible from the house; this way, visitors would be emotionally stirred when they stumbled upon the unexpected and beautiful feature as a grand finale to a garden tour. Wherever it's situated, a crevice garden tends to slow traffic down and break up sight-lines with its detail and complexity.

Your crevice garden can be sited to stand alone, away from features that detract from its mountain-like bulk. In a lawn, for example, it will be the tallest and most prominent feature. Such a site makes it possible for the top of the crevice garden to feel as though it's touching the sky when seen from the lowest angle, visually setting the rocks and plants against dark, incoming storm systems or clouds illuminated at sunset. Because it is a gain in elevation, it will tend to divide the open space, giving it a greater sense of bulk. But wherever you choose to place your outcrop, avoid symmetry and equality; consider the sizes of the resulting spaces and aim to make them different.

Positioning a crevice garden alone in a field of turf creates an 'island' effect. If you don't want that, build transitional zones or consider transforming part or all of the turf into a meadow, gravel garden, or extension of adjacent perennial gardens. A nearby meadow or perennial bed is also very useful to the rock gardener, serving as a repository for pruned material in the spirit of the 'chop and drop' method – you can even just brush debris off the crevice to be absorbed by the meadow.

Gravel gardens, featuring varied gravel sizes and a few stones, or with a little of their own gently undulating topography, are a great natural extension to the crevice. Make one deep enough and you will have a scree garden, a perfect complement and contrast to the nearby outcrop.

An island effect is created when the outcrop is situated alone in a large open area, such as an expanse of lawn.

As a general rule, grow taller herbaceous plants and bulbs in flat areas adjacent to the outcrop, not on the outcrop itself.

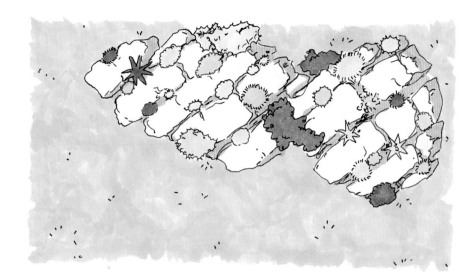

Site your crevice garden
off-center in its space for
movement, life, and naturalism.

A contrast of hard and soft
elements helps to create
a beautiful tension in the
crevice garden.

A water feature such as a pond or waterfall
adds vitality to the scene.

The nature of a crevice garden affects how it relates to nearby objects, hard and soft. It is a solid, opaque, often massive entity, which will have an affinity with nearby hard elements such as paving stones, patios, walls, and boulders but will contrast well with the garden's soft features – leaves, turf, ground covers, trees and shrubs. This becomes more apparent in winter when hard structures take precedence. Balance hard and soft to your liking, because the tension between them might be one of the most internally compelling things about your garden space. The stark impact of a new crevice garden will soften as the tiny plants mature and the inanimate, hard surfaces and textures become engulfed with the softness of the living vegetation.

A crevice garden can be so loud it halts you in your tracks, blocks a view, breaks up a space, and casts long shadows. Bright, sun-kissed peaks can stop the wind, create a snowdrift, or make more room for cliff-hanger plants, all the while raising a mineral fist against the sky.

Ponds, waterfalls, streams, and seeps always draw the viewer's attention, invoking a sense of calm and peace, but in the crevice garden, water must integrate with the story of the stone – remember that over time water tends to create round stones, so numerous sharp, fresh stones won't integrate successfully. Few crevice gardens have been designed incorporating water features, but they offer opportunities for brand-new microclimates.

From an aesthetic point of view, rock gardens are more readily sited on slopes. Taking advantage of this, a crevice garden flanking each side of a stairway or sloping path will show off rocks and plants while keeping an open, airy aesthetic.

Practical points

Don't

Don't place tons of crevice garden on top of your buried utilities, which may need replacing sooner than you think.

Avoid making a path too narrow for foot traffic and a lawnmower.

Avoid siting near rhizomatous plants.

Aim to

Be aware of stormwater runoff and the snow from adjacent land, roofs, and downspouts. Don't accidentally dam water against your house!

Do

Put it near a path where you can see its tiny plants without binoculars.

Site the garden safely away from the scraping of your neighborhood streetside snowplow.

At the Cheyenne Botanic Gardens in Wyoming, above and opposite, where common blizzards bring heavy snow, surface drainage from a very large greenhouse had to be diverted around the crevice garden and released to a sidewalk; otherwise both the roof and garden runoff would have been trapped against the building. A quick thaw in late winter could make for a great deal of water suddenly needing a place to go. It was accepted that one part of the crevice garden would be regularly pummeled by snow falling 9m (30ft) from the roof in winter, limiting the plant possibilities in that area to those that can survive a beating.

Next pages: Where there could have been a boring retaining wall, there is instead a crevice garden and seep feature at Juniper Level Botanic Garden, North Carolina.

73

Trees and the crevice garden

Trees are not exactly good neighbors to crevice gardens. They tend to make an outcrop look smaller, detracting from its bulk and mass, and they also compete with its plants, both above and below ground. Overhanging trees will drop leaves, needles, spent flowers, and other debris, which no alpine plant will appreciate. Fallen leaves can become hiding places for bugs, fungi and disease, as well as slowly adding unwanted humus to your crevice garden soil. In fact, your crevice garden's health will rely in part on your being armed with a leaf blower. Furthermore, nearby trees may send roots that grow upward, and are usually faster to take up water and nutrients than most rock garden plants. Some are even allelopathic, using their own chemicals to kill or subdue neighboring plants.

To reduce the amount of tree root invasion, use metal flashing or plastic root barriers designed for roofing or containing bamboo usually to a depth of 45cm (18in) or more. Aim for a single, uninterrupted barrier, as overlapping segments have penetrable weak spots. This also works to defend crevice gardens from the invasion of neighboring aggressive or rhizomatous plants or weeds. In extreme cases, where the soil under the garden is infested with tree roots or perennial weeds, a heavy-duty geotextile can be laid over the native soil before introducing the crevice media. This was the case in the famous crevice garden at the Montreal Botanical Gardens.

Perhaps the worst effect of trees is that they cast shade, something that rock garden plants generally don't want, though it can prove useful for certain plants during the afternoon summer heat. Under a deciduous tree in winter, sun will reach the plants, desirable or not. Very thirsty trees, and especially conifers, can be used to shelter dry-loving plants from excessive natural moisture.

Crevice gardens work well in troughs.

Crevices in troughs

Saxatile plants have been grown in reused livestock troughs for more than a century, liberating small plants from the crowded garden with its roots and earthworms and bringing them nearer the viewer. Troughs allow for any soil media and small ones can easily be moved for protection. They even offer the opportunity to use a different rock type to the rest of the garden. A trough will be drier than its contextual garden and may need irrigation. Orient rocks at an angle for naturalism, and consider letting a rock overlap the edge of the container. Just make sure the container has adequate drainage holes.

Top: The sleek, modern edges of this raised concrete planter are softened with rocks and saxifrages.

Right: In the spirit of historical paintings, allow a trough rock to 'break the picture plane'. In larger gardens it could hang over a sidewalk edge, above, or even a small container, below.

This trough of saxifrages in tufa has a dramatic height to width ratio of one-third.

78 Crevice garden size

Everything good a crevice garden can do, it will do better if it's bigger. This is important for collectors who quickly run out of room, even though they are collecting tiny plants. Overall, just maximize what you have.

Bring your crevice garden up to an edge of its allotted area to kiss paths, or to hug your house's foundation, so that it can have its maximum breadth, rather than be an isolated feature within a narrow border. Be deliberate in considering its footprint. One great trick is to emulate the lines of the stones you'll use, even copying the shape of an actual stone in your pile.

Aim for the height of the garden to be roughly a third of its width. Taller than this can look artificial; if it is shorter, you will miss the advantages of shadows, microclimates, and the sheer volume of planting spaces. But at the same time, in a dry climate, when conserving moisture is more important than drainage, a low-profile mound will be more functional. Use a light, mobile object such as a bag of leaves or a sheet over lawn furniture to mock-up the height and volume you want so that you gain an idea of how it will look in your garden.

All rules are meant to be broken, as exemplified by these tufa columns designed by Dutch rock gardener Harry Jans, which have a tiny footprint relative to height.

Make sure your outcrop has an asymmetrical footprint like this one belonging to Cameron Kidd.

Form and shape

A crevice garden's presence is also manifested in its form, which for naturalism should always embrace asymmetry because it looks more alive, like a person in *contrapposto* with their weight on one foot and a tilt to hips and shoulders.

Each single outcrop should look like a solid rock which was revealed when soil eroded away, with a unified form. A second or third mound, with a path or space between them, ties a dramatic crevice garden into an existing garden rather than it appearing as an isolated, even inappropriate feature. While standing on that path, you will be immersed in the garden rather than observing it from the outside.

A garden can be one big harmonious unit, or broken up into pieces. The former's strength is volume, presence, and mass; the latter has more microclimates, variety, and dynamism, which slows the viewer down. Pick what you like, and find your own balance between variety and harmony.

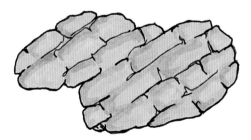
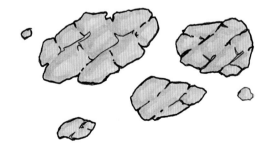

A single unified form, left, versus a broken up form that is integrated into the landscape, right.

Drama comes in many forms, from deep valleys to sharp peaks. Even a flat, lower expanse can serve to contrast the high points and can emulate meadows or plains. For the high points, maximize drama by building a miniature mountain that looks difficult to climb, requiring technical mountaineering skills, terrifying ascents, and long rappels, with ridges to traverse and canyons to navigate. If you have two peaks, definitely make one higher than the other. The same goes for cliff heights, distances between focal points, and depths of valleys. In European public gardens, there is a historical tradition of creating rock garden mounds by digging a pond close by. If that pond were not full of water, however, this would create a double-sized slope going from the top of the hill to literally below ground – a trick that could be used in even a small space.

Variety in height and slope will create wetter and drier areas. A valley under a slope can physically trap water for a moment before it carries on, creating those sought-after 'moist but well-drained' conditions. In dry climates where retaining water is important, a lower profile mound may be preferable, and one whose form will trap water instead of shed it all.

You can choose which character of the rock to exaggerate: in the top illustration, the sharp sides of rocks are exposed to create an angular, jagged garden, while in the lower one, the rounder sides of the same rocks produce a smoother effect.

Below: Varying slopes and forms will create high points, bringing layers of interesting features. Any feature can be echoed, which lends a sense of space and belonging.

Juniper Level Botanic Garden in North Carolina is an example of a post-apocalyptic design using recycled concrete.

The planted spheres of Utrecht Botanic Gardens.

Human and apocalyptic designs

Concrete that was once a home driveway was cut and recycled into modernist cubes at this crevice at the Aurora Water-wise Garden in Colorado.

A garden that is not intended to emulate nature can be as crazy as its maker wants and break all rules for naturalism, but must adhere to another sort of aesthetic order and logic. The laws of physics, stability, and plant growth also need to remain. Some makers of crevice gardens are fascinated by the abandoned city of Chernobyl, where trees and shrubs eat at the old town through cracks in the asphalt. Ruin gardens and concrete crevice gardens follow this post-modern intuition of decay. They promote thoughts such as: 'What does a street or sidewalk look like when an agave grows up in the middle of it?' Or, 'Where will the post-apocalyptic blue gentians pop up when they repopulate the cobbled streets of alpine towns?'

Above: Perhaps the most novel crevice system to date is Peter Korn's at Klinta Trädgård in Skåne, southern Sweden, using styrofoam blocks on a roof to create a lightweight and insulative crevice environment, beneficially merging two unlikely bedfellows: green roofs and crevice gardens.

Right: Traditionally, crevice gardens have not used mortar, but at Denver Botanic Gardens, the obelisk's interiors are mortared while the exteriors are filled with a clay and seed slurry for plants to grow in. When a design does not reflect nature, it can break many rules, but the rules of good composition and physics are still in effect.

Rock shape and color

Generally, the stone shapes that are easiest to work with are neither perfectly square nor perfectly round. It also helps if they feature two roughly parallel sides that facilitate the orientation. You can use any kind of stone you want, though as a general rule, design begs that different types of rock should not be mixed in one garden. Look for a type whose color will complement the plants you want, or match existing stone, walls, gravel, or other hardscapes. But take care, Kenton once realized to his dismay that his beloved silver plants were completely invisible against a favourite silver-colored stone.

Light-colored stone reflects heat and will cool nearby soil but darker stone absorbs heat and will warm adjacent soil. The stone color you choose may also be based on your garden, home, or nearby scenery. This also applies to shape. Sharp stones appear active and dramatic, while more rounded ones look restful and calm. A landscape already featuring angular boulders will meld better with a crevice garden that continues that theme. You may discover a stunningly beautiful type of stone, one that has potential to upstage your plants. Address this by either ensuring that the variety of plants you grow is even more interesting, making the stone look unified by comparison, or by using the plants to provide harmony with repeated colors, forms, or species to frame and quilt your wild, beautiful stone together.

If you are using a pre-existing pile of mixed rock, work with the most common and relatable pieces, casting off the outliers, burying them, or hiding their incongruous faces in favor of the sides that honor the common or most desired character. In the end, economy and realism decide which stone you will use. It's wise to source a stone that is common in your area or from an active quarry so you can get more of it should you run short or want to expand in future. Sourcing from a quarry also increases the likelihood of acquiring matching gravel for the top-dressing.

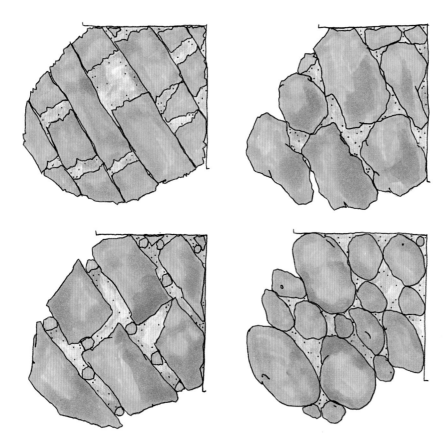

Irregularly shaped stones, such as these two examples on the right, create crevices automatically, while regular, brick-like stones, shown in the two examples left, must be spaced intentionally to provide them.

Rock size

A few large rocks are important for creating the broad, steep cliff faces, an important component in achieving high drama. Large rocks are also useful for hiding ugly vertical joints, where the ends of two slabs sometimes meet awkwardly. Large rocks give instant height, from which plants can hang, then use medium-sized rocks that you feel comfortable carrying and working with for much of the garden. Lastly, you'll need just as many smaller stones to fill in, graduating down to gravel and chips for the top-dressing. A small crevice garden can use a single large rock to anchor it and a handful of smaller ones for the rest of the garden.

Gravels for top-dressing

Ideally, your gravel will be made of the same material as the outcrop, mimicking what happens in nature as material from the parent rock is actively weathered and strewn about the surface. In a perfect world, you'll be able to harvest the pieces that have broken off larger rocks during transport to use as your top-dressing. Even fairly large gravel pieces can be used, blurring the line between the top-dressing and the deeply sunken rocks, resulting in a very natural look. In general, avoid round, pea-shaped gravel as a top-dressing. It is a natural result of erosion from stream bottoms rather than rocky slopes, and it rolls off a garden's cliffs and can be a dangerous slipping hazard on paths. Crushed or sharp gravel has angles that lock together, helping it to stay on the garden where it belongs.

While a common, practical average for top-dressing depth is roughly 2.5cm (1in), allow yourself thickly and thinly top-dressed areas for different plants. A thicker layer will prevent the germination of both weeds and your own plants, so choose those spots deliberately. Consider even leaving some bare soil areas – not only does this indeed happen in nature, but it is appealing to beneficial insects like solitary bees for their tiny earthen dwellings.

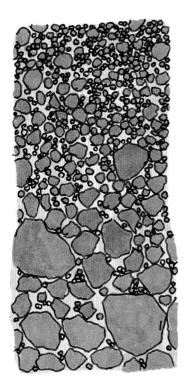

A variety of gravel sizes is key for a natural look.

Types of stone

The stone that you chose for your crevice garden will be one of the strongest determinants of its character and behavior. For some design goals and easy plants it may make little to no difference, but for others it may be critical.

Permeable stone
Natural shales, sandstones, limestone, and tufa are permeable to some degree and affect how water and temperature work in the garden. These highly valued stones will shed excess water, like any other stone, but will also absorb some water, helping to keep plant roots more evenly moist and cool during dry periods.

Water also affects temperature. Its thermal mass (temperature storage) is three or four times greater than the stone itself. When conditions are right, a permeable stone can create evaporative cooling.

Beware of some sandstones, shale, and mudstones, which may be so soft they erode and fall apart in just a few years.

Stratified types of stone are the most commonly used in crevice gardens.

Stratified stone
Stratified, which are usually sedimentary, stones are most commonly used in classic crevice gardens, as their roughly parallel sides lend well to creating and controlling the form of a tall and freestanding garden, with crevices running their entire length and depth. These planes also tend to be flat, which means much of each stone is buried when it is stood on end, creating the deepest root-run possible and accommodating the greatest number of plants per square meter. It's pleasing when the ends of the stones are variable or weathered as these 'faces' are seen from outside the garden and create its shape and character.

Slate is technically a metamorphic stone with thin, even layers that afford maximum crevice spaces, so it's a favorite for crevice gardens. Some gneiss and schist also share these characteristics. Many other stratified stones are flat and plate-like, allowing for the tallest constructions on a small footprint.

Hard stones
Volcanic stones, including a colorful and diverse cast of granite, gneiss, schist, basalt, rhyolite, and others, are hard and their angles of breakage (geologic cleavage) are irregular. The way they break is determined by their mineral components and crystalline structure and they are usually mined by blasting. Because these are highly versatile stones, a designer can choose to feature sharp or softer faces. They pose a bigger challenge in choosing a pattern to constrain the design but offer broader options for the final outcome.

Round stones
The spaces formed between round stones will be triangular and amorphously shaped rather than the regular slot-like crevices between rectangular stones. Round rock cannot create a crevice garden as tall or with actual crevices as deep, but they still function. The normal rules of angle and orientation cannot be applied here, as they have neither flat nor parallel surfaces. The trick is to ensure a variety of stone sizes, from large all the way down to a fine gravel top-dressing. Also make sure you have more than one rock of the most colorful or outstanding stone type, should they be multi-colored river rock: if it sticks out like a sore thumb, either remove it or repeat it.

There are particularly beautiful round stones in nature because they've literally been polished. Round stones are also usually cheap, since they are plentiful near rivers and beaches. The inviting roundness of these stones is safer for children and gardeners too and they echo the shape of a bun plant. Are they rock-shaped plants or plant-shaped rocks?

Round stones evoke rivers, glaciers, or wind-swept deserts.

Tufa

Tufa is a light and porous calcareous stone formed when water that has seeped through limestone begins to deposit calcium carbonate, which rapidly accumulates to form soft, porous, tan-colored travertine. It can increase so rapidly that it can overtake undecayed organic material. Leaves, twigs, dead animals, and even beer cans have been found embedded in tufa. Its amazing plant-growing ability lies in its offering of air, water, and nutrients – an accidentally ideal matrix for a plant's rhizosphere. Tufa also boasts a high pH, making it a highly desirable medium for lime-loving plants. Tufa is typically used to grow plants directly in the rock itself, often on its truly vertical surfaces, and the plantable crevices in between rock are a bonus.

Mixing stone types

If you decide to deviate from using just one kind of stone, consider mimicking a natural occurrence of commingling. Some builders of crevice gardens have created a vein of a different stone running between courses of the predominant stone, mimicking either a volcanic intrusion within a metamorphic matrix or a sedimentary layer laid there during a different geologic episode.

Other materials

So much uncharted territory begs to be explored! The only limitation of material suitable in a crevice garden is that it is hard enough, survives the elements, and doesn't kill your plants. One new favorite is broken concrete, sometimes affectionately nicknamed 'urbanite', which is widely available and, as a recycled material, highly sustainable. Broken concrete can be found for free almost everywhere, and usually has slab-like shapes featuring two parallel sides that work well for the creation of deep crevices. As it is made of limy materials, it can provide a higher pH – generally better for saxatile plants – and be used by gardeners otherwise limited by acidic soils.

87

Tony Stireman's north-facing tufa crevice garden employs evaporative cooling, hosting alpines which may otherwise have cooked in the semi-arid valley climate of Salt Lake City, Utah.

Crevice gardeners covet tufa. Here, saxifrage roots grow right through it and into the soil below.

The orientation of strata

One of the first questions crevice gardens prompt is, 'Why the lines?' We call them 'strata' because they mimic the natural stratification of sedimentary or metamorphosed stone, which has been subjected to tectonic forces and tilted from its original horizontal position to varying angles up to 90 degrees. As in bricklaying, the stones forming one of those lines is called a 'course'. In a garden, the strata provide a unifying framework implying that all the stones were once one big stone that has cleaved, cracked, and weathered over time. It is also a structural framework that allows the freedom to build high, low, and everywhere in between.

Most crevice gardens emulate natural strata by orienting them to a predetermined cardinal direction, kept consistent by the use of a compass. The most natural look is to place the strata running at an angle at least 15 degrees off adjacent artificial lines.

When deciding the orientation of the strata, consider the microclimates the plants need, and what you want. For example, if you desire a maximum number of crevices facing the cooler and wetter north, then your strata should be running north–south with a high point closer to the south end of the outcrop, creating a steep south face, and a longer and more gradual north slope which will provide a greater north-facing surface area. If you're building strictly for aesthetics, consider the direction from which the garden will be viewed most frequently. It is possible, but tricky, to bend or curve the strata instead of following a compass-oriented line. This is fun and attention-grabbing, but difficult to do well.

Below: Juniper Level Botanic Garden follows its own rules with playful strata lines that swerve and collide.

For natural effect, top, orient the strata oblique to nearby straight lines. This rule doesn't apply for non-natural styles, bottom.

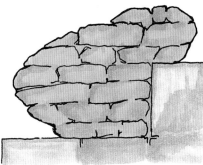

Left: Oriented strata unify a crevice garden, creating the effect of a natural outcrop.

Orient strata at oblique angles to existing straight lines including container walls.

Sun

Sun

Consider the microclimate your plants need and then design the strata and shape of your mound to amplify your desired aspect, a south preference above or a north preference below (for Northern Hemisphere gardens).

Do you prefer viewing rocks from their sides, top picture, or their ends, above? This may affect your choice regarding strata orientation.

Right: Narrow footprints and orientation as seen from above. Counterintuitively, a long, skinny footprint is more structurally sound and can be built taller with strata somewhat perpendicular to its length (left). With strata running lengthwise (right), the stones will have to be buried very deeply to sustain any height.

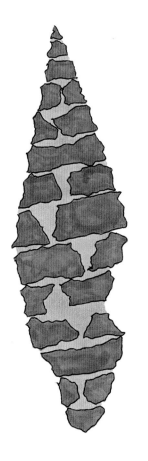

Paul Cumbleton has bent strata artistically instead of following a compass-oriented line, which gives him crevices facing all aspects in his garden in Somerset, UK.

Here the strata are laid obliquely in relation to the nearby house and this, combined with their slightly leaning tilt, generate great drama and movement in a tiny garden.

The angle of tilt

Crevice gardens don't always have to conform to the classic vertical rock placement. Artistically minded rock gardeners need to feel no boundaries when placing rock as long as the basic principles of design and construction are followed so that plants find the cracks and crevices they need for successful growth. The following examples compare the strengths, limitations, and possibilities in using diagonal and horizontal tilts as well as the traditional vertical style. The angle you choose is up to your visual and botanical needs; you can take inspiration from the region where your rocks were 'born'.

This garden features boulders set at angles of roughly 45 degrees.

Vertical arrangement

In the classic or 'Czech' style, the crevice garden emulates the dramatic look of stratified rock that has been geologically heaved upward so that the layers are standing at an angle of about 90 degrees. This vertical stratification offers the greatest control over form, size, and steepness. It's also the easiest to build. You can start from any side of the garden, and add to or subtract from it easily. Vertical construction allows for maximum height in a small area, and can be a simple solution to steep grade changes. It's easy to predict how water will move in vertical construction, as surface water is quickly directed into the crevices from the exposed, upward-facing rocks. Vertical construction also buries most of the rocks, promoting extensive and far-reaching root systems.

Diagonal tilt

Natural outcrops of diagonal strata embody dynamic forces by revealing active geologic pressure. This adds a breath of life to a garden, giving you a chance to replicate what geologists measure as 'strike and dip'.

With gently tilted strata, each view of the sides of a crevice garden is vastly different, giving you a variety of surfaces to admire and plant. However, it's more difficult to build a tilted crevice garden, especially if it's on an acute angle, since one layer of stone is literally leaning on the next. During construction, you have to keep track of the orientation of the layers, as well as monitoring the angle at which they lean.

Severely tilted rock placement demands either aggregate in the soil mix or the use of spacer stones to prevent crevice space from being crushed. The pitched-roof effect of this high-angle construction also redirects water in less predictable ways, since every stone is a strong slope.

Horizontal tilt

Horizontal rock placement aesthetically honors outcroppings of low-angle sedimentary rock and the dry-stacked rock wall. It must use gravity, simple physics, and careful arrangement to hold together without mortar. Many plants, such as campanulas, sedums, and sempervivums, have long been grown in dry-stacked walls which originally had an entirely practical purpose. Sometimes, the plants self-sow into the cracks, transforming the wall into a garden.

Tipping a wall's entire vertical face into a slope is more structurally sound than keeping it perfectly level and capitalizes on the runoff diversion. This subtle tilt, referred to by wall-builders as the 'batter', has a plant-friendly side effect in that the spaces between the rocks are better able to retain soil and water rather than shedding it off the surface. With little of its face receiving rain, a wall can be extremely dry relative to the ground around it, an advantage in a wet climate, and one of the rare opportunities to have a completely rain-blocking overhang.

Arguably, patios and pathways with pavers or flagstones are two-dimensional horizontal crevice gardens as well. When paving stones are set in sand, as they generally are, they offer conditions similar to crevice gardens. It's not uncommon to see the rare and glorious gems of the crevice garden reseed into the humble stone path below, often growing better there.

Horizontal orientation may require spacers or gravel to preserve useful, uncrushed space between layers; the same is true for going diagonal.

Rock walls, like those of this raised bed at Munich Botanical Garden, are functional crevice gardens.

Crevice width and depth

A crevice is simply a gap between adjacent stones filled with a light, porous medium where plant roots can take hold. Generally, 2.5cm (1 in) is a functional and practical crevice width, being narrow enough to direct roots deeply and wide enough to plant. Close crevices encourage deep rooting, sending the roots down to where moisture and temperature are more consistent. A 2.5cm (1in) crevice will also fit most rock garden digging tools and the common 5cm (2in) nursery pot. Many saxatile plants are chasmophytes – or crevice-lovers – evolved to grow in the tightest of cracks with no soil at all. For these, you may want to create deep, paper-thin crevices.

The depth of the crevice is a result of how deeply the rocks are buried. The deeper the better, but aim for at least 20cm (8in). This gives most plants a comfortable permanent rhizosphere, yet is shallow enough that roots can grow through it within one season, if they prefer. You may wince at burying the bulk of your beautiful, expensive stones, but don't forget that much of their magic goes on underground.

Generally, you'll get maximum benefit by filling crevices to their brim. This results in a more unified look, optimizes surface drainage, and inhibits pooling. Debris is less likely to settle and linger, requiring less time to clean the garden. Finally, a topped-up crevice maximally exposes plants at the surface and encourages them to grow into a neat, symmetrical shape.

That said, open or sunken crevices have their place. These catch and direct moisture, which is beneficial in dry climates and for plants that need more water. Furthermore, the plants down in those gaps are shaded by the stones as the angle of the sun changes and also hold an insulating cover of snow. Other advantages of such crevices is that they create a special microclimate for marginally hardy plants and force plants to conform to their shape, resulting in quirky and unique plant forms that would not occur if the plant grew uninhibited. In gardens of this style, every stone must be more deeply buried to be stable, and the overall appearance will not necessarily look like one solid mass or outcrop.

A garden can have both kinds of crevice, where the solid, level ones are in the interior of an outcrop, and the sunken, shadowy crevices are along an edge as though they are part of a cliff that is actively eroding.

To make a bigger planting pocket for a dwarf shrub or clump of bulbs without weakening the construction, leave a gap like a missing brick in a wall; the exposed soil can be masked with top-dressing or a veneer stone.

The crevice garden at Yampa Botanic Gardens contains nothing but open crevices, which required builder Ryan Keating to bury each stone deeply for stability against traffic and frost-heaving. This ameliorates the effects of the climate allowing the garden to host plants that would usually struggle in Steamboat Springs, Colorado.

A garden can host a variety of crevice depths or even soil mix types without affecting its appearance.

Edges

The edge of a crevice garden is where most human interaction will happen, so give its design some thought. A dynamic garden will have both rocky cliff edges that return dramatically to ground level, and soft edges that fade more gently into the existing landscape gradient. This softening can be done with plants or by setting the edge stones far enough apart for them to be no longer creating tight crevices. The stone's edges should always be well buried (usually half their volume) and return to the ground level in a pleasing way that implies a continuing mass of rock underground.

A good crevice garden features both gentle vegetated returns (left) as well as steep, exposed returns (right).

Below: Steep, tall edges bring plants closer to eye level at Montreal Botanic Gardens.

Steep, tall edges bring plants close to eye level. You can also allow stones to escape the bed or slightly overhang a path, which makes the garden jump out at passersby. Building the crevice garden right to the edge of a path also increases its overall footprint.

Paths

Form follows function when it comes to garden paths. Will the path need to deliver a steady stream of viewers? Or will it be a small goat trail, travelled occasionally by a gardener for maintenance purposes? Large, level paths are essential where golf carts, snowplows and wheelchairs will have access and allow people to pass by one another. In public places, paths must meet structural requirements for width and grade, often to satisfy building codes or liability concerns.

As a general rule, straighter or wider paths speed up the travel of visitors while narrow zigzagged ones slow them down, drawing their attention to details in the garden. Paths that meander between and around outcrops allow viewing from all sides as well as immersing visitors in the environment. Many public gardens use big paths for public thoroughfares, nearly invisible ones for gardeners, and narrow ones to siphon traffic from a quieter corner of the garden back to its center. Paths are also the throughline of the story and provide the order in which a visitor experiences the garden, so reconnecting loops encourage viewers to notice new things.

Concrete and other impermeable paths are heavy and unforgiving, creating a prevailing aesthetic hardness. They also shed rainwater, creating wet microclimates where they drain. Some gardeners pave their pathways with the same rock used in the garden, maintaining the orientation of the strata in

The backyard Czech gardeners, especially Stanislav Čepička, construct paths as tightly as possible, even forcing visitors to step over raised rocks now and again, yet still somehow allowing just enough room for two people to pass.

the outcrop and emulating a human-made road-cut. This is a lot of work and requires appropriate flat-edged rock so that the 'pavement' does not pose a tripping hazard for pedestrians.

A cheaper, less labor-intensive option is to pave the access paths with gravel or stone chips that can be raked flat. A little variety in the gravel size will instantly make it look natural, like fragments that have broken off rocks above, especially when some loose rock is nestled at the edge of the path against the stone cliffs.

This New Zealand garden has a sturdy, level path paved with stones placed vertically and in alignment with the garden, but with tops that make a flat surface for walking. Its advantages are stability, supporting the edge of the outcrop, as well as inviting reseeding plants which like a low crevice, maximizing plant space while allowing visitors to literally walk on crevices to see the garden.

Keep clearance of irrigation spray heads in mind when placing them so that their streams are not blocked by tall rocks.

Irrigation

One of the great strengths of the crevice garden is that the roots of plants are forced deep between the stones where they find steady moisture, so irrigation is not required in many climates except during establishment of the plants and in periods of hot, dry weather. The best way to minimize irrigation is to understand the climate of origin of the plants that you want to grow. Irrigation may be necessary if you want to grow alpine gems that aren't accustomed to drought, but in wet climates drainage will be a far more important factor than irrigation.

A crevice garden should be 'hydro-zoned' with respect to surrounding areas. A tiny garden can simply get what the rest of the garden gets, but a large one deserves its own irrigation zone and treatment. Generally, large-droplet overhead watering is best to mimic rain and capitalize on the water diversion of the surface of the stones. This is ideally delivered from the outside of the garden with big sprayers shooting in, but occasionally you might need a head installed in the middle of a larger bed. 'Pop-ups' and 'rotors' work well because they look like nothing more than a big black button at rest but can rise to 30cm (12in) or more when they do their work. Slow delivery, or low GPH (gallons per hour) heads are preferable,

again because they replicate rain and don't cause undue erosion. Heads should always be arranged with 'head-to-head coverage', meaning that their spray patterns overlap. Keep the height of the garden, big rocks, and growing plants in mind when placing heads so that the trajectory of water isn't blocked – it's very common for a corner of a garden to become fatally dry because a plant grew up and blocked the head that serviced that area.

Drip irrigation or even buried internal irrigation can also work, but while the latter keeps all unsightly plastic hidden, it may be inaccessible if it clogs or fails. There is no perfect system, just the best fit for a job. Leave as much repair access as possible, ideally running irrigation lines in a mulched path that is easily dug up. Save yourself a load of trouble and bury a heavy-duty sleeve pipe if you think there is even the remotest chance you will want to run any kind of utility or water line under a crevice garden in the future.

Adjusting your irrigation schedule is the first part of managing how much your plants grow (and need pruning) as well as how many weeds you attract. It becomes a part of the long-term conversation you'll have with your garden.

SOIL AND PLANTS

The soil is home to half of a plant, and while it is not the pretty portion, an appropriate soil is critical. The big advantage to creating a new soil medium for a rock garden is that you can grow plants you couldn't grow before. Experiment, observe, and learn from mistakes. Try new mixes to find something that 'just feels right' in the hand. In general, crevice garden media should emulate undeveloped wild soils of open texture and high porosity, where historical vegetation has not accumulated to create humus. This means you'll use compost lightly, or only in specific areas and for the plants that require it.

To begin, learn what type of native soil you have. You may use it for the whole garden or only as the foundation under new media. Most likely, your existing soil will be covered with imported sand or another mix, but their relationship and interaction is important. Keep in mind that most media will settle over time, requiring crevices to be topped up in future years.

This crevice garden in Victoria, British Columbia uses a sandy, well-drained soil mix over a deeper layer of clay loam.

Choosing a mix

Most good mixes have two to four ingredients of differing qualities. One mix may be a miracle for one plant but kill another, so don't be wedded to a single solution. Play around and make small test batches. For growing new plants, you'll probably continue to adjust what you use, especially with changes in material availability or the type of plant you are currently obsessing over.

In wet, humid climates, gardeners can get away with loose mixes that readily drain because they never experience dry spells. The humidity is high enough that the evaporation rate from the soil slows. In most climates, pure sharp sand at a minimum depth of 10cm (4in) has been a proven mainstay medium, used alone. If this sounds too extreme, try roughly 80 percent coarse-grained sand and 20 percent raw loam with some amount of humus. This generally ensures that the sand dominates the soil structure but there is not quite enough garden loam to clog its pores.

In steppe and desert climates receiving less than 600mm (24in) of annual precipitation, pure sand as well as equal parts sand and gravel work brilliantly for irrigated alpine-focused gardens. However, if it's not irrigated much, or is intended to grow xeric (dryland) plants, coarse sand alone is too extreme, drying out too much even for cacti. Use pure gravel fines, decomposed granite or silty or sandy loam, as long as it is lighter than, or equal in texture to, the earth it's sitting on and has little or no compost added. If equal density, it allows deep ground-water to percolate upwards through capillary action. You can further adjust the key ingredient of your soil with material additives.

Providing nutrition

Rock garden plants can be roughly categorized into two groups: those that like organic humus in the soil and those that don't. If you are aiming to grow cliff-dwelling chasmophytes such as *Saxifraga*, *Lewisia*, and *Draba*, or dryland plants such as cacti, *Eriogonum*, and *Penstemon*, aim for a mineral mix with no compost. Others, such as *Gentiana*, *Rhodiola*, *Primula*, and *Galanthus*, which tend to grow on walkable, gently sloping wild turf or tundra, want plenty of compost in their soil. Most gardeners use a mineral soil in the main body of the crevice garden but have an organic side, pocket, slope, or section at a low spot.

Almost any native soil will supply mineral nutrition, as will most natural gravel, aggregate, or sand. A basic soil mix of equal parts crushed gravel and 'masonry' or 'concrete' sand (with finer particles) is one of the most adaptable mediums, usable in the wettest and driest climates – but only if it's irrigated. The sand is the basic matrix, but the gravel lends a little more stability and any rock dust will contribute nutrition. Some gardeners will cut their native soil with sand, again half and half, then test it to ensure it will drain. Whenever native soil is in your mix, take the time to screen out perennial weed roots such as couch grass and bindweed, which are almost impossible to remove once established in the crevices.

Depth and type of mix in the crevice

Your chosen medium can make up the main body of the garden or be used only to fill the spaces between rocks which are sitting on your natural soil. In a wet climate it's generally more useful to go for the former choice, and in a dry climate the latter. Variety of depth will give you options in future.

There are two precautions to heed when introducing a new soil. First, avoid letting fine-textured material, especially clay, clog the pores. Clay's very fine particles are hundreds of times smaller than sand and can effectively clog and eliminate their porosity.

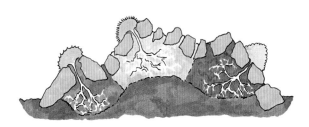

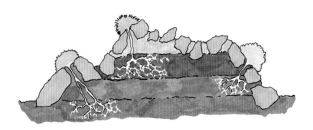

A garden can host a variety of soil mix types without its appearance being affected.

The Goldilocks cake: soils in layers

Some preach against layered soil, because any interface between two soils slows the transfer of water and nutrients and may inhibit roots from entering a deeper layer. However, layered soils do occur in nature – in glacial moraines, for example, where the path of water is fast and vertical through the top layers, then slow and more lateral toward the bottom. This creates open, oxygenated, dry soil up above and wet, saturated soil beneath, allowing plants to choose where to grow roots.

If there is leftover on-site native soil from another project, or from digging in your largest stones, that is best used as a bottom layer – a great way to bulk up the garden and save some money on materials in the process. The most important rule to follow in making soil layers is that heavier soil with a higher capillarity, for example clay, should always sit below lighter soils, such as sand, otherwise a perched water table will form. In this case, heavy soil on top must be completely saturated before it releases water to the next layer, possibly drowning plants in the process. For this reason, ironically, the time-held advice to put gravel or shards in the bottom of a pot for drainage actually has the opposite outcome! We'd be better off making a wick for water to escape the pot's bottom holes.

Also note that layers create a one-way street for water's travel in the soil. Moisture held in lower, denser layers of higher capillarity will not be released to layers above. This is a problem if the majority of your plants' roots are within an upper mix and it gets too dry, but deep-rooted plants that bypass a dry layer will be fine, or the dry layer can be used as an advantage in a wet climate. This effect can actually help to manage saline (or 'alkali' as they are known in the US) soils common in arid regions by preventing natural salts from moving upward. In dry climates, layered soils also store water deeply, away from the hot, fast-drying surface. In any climate, creating a drier-than-normal surface through soil layering reduces weeds and makes saxatile plants happy.

In your garden, the nuances of the behavior of water in the soils will reveal themselves: in time, every plant in your crevice garden will find soil that's not too wet or too dry, but just right.

Pockets and patches

The most advanced crevice gardens perform a variety of functions for plants with microclimates above and a variety of soil types below. Such soil pockets can be just enough for a single plant or wide enough to qualify as an open bed on their own between stone-heavy areas. It happens in nature in scree piles, moist meadows, and even alpine turf zones amid the rockiest places.

Keep in mind how the soil of a pocket or bed interacts with the surrounding soil. Whether you use no additional soil, a single soil mix, several basic soil textures in layers, or a collection of varied pockets, a well-designed crevice garden is a complex water highway that routes water, delivering moisture where it's needed and shedding moisture where it's not. All the while, a good soil ecosystem preserves air and oxygen in the depths for your precious plants.

Paul Cumbleton experiments continually with customized soil pockets and grows the elusive *Castilleja latifolia* in Somerset, UK.

Some soil mixes may be of such loose materials that they flow like sand in an hourglass. In pots, place a screen of inorganic material such as wire or plastic mesh in the bottom to prevent soil from escaping the drainage holes. In the crevice garden, you can mix in 10mm (1/2in) sized gravel to an equal part soil in areas under and around unstable crevices, and the gravel will work to dam erosion. A clay puck used to mortar stones into these steep crevices will achieve the same result.

Settling and aging

Disturbed soil will inevitably settle, most prevalently among the outside stones of the garden, which sit directly on the disturbed original soil. Stockpile some of your mix during construction to top up these sunken crevices. The greatest settling usually happens the first winter in cold climates or in the first rainy season in wet climates. Long-term settling means the air spaces in the soil have reduced, and gravels or aggregates might find their way to the surface, leaving behind organic matter that will break down. Expect 33 percent sinkage from a garden mix comprising one-third compost, even if it takes as long as ten years in a dry climate.

Containers especially suffer when the soil becomes 'tired'. Not only does the texture relax as organics collapse, but nutrients become depleted and literally wash away. You can alleviate the resulting poor aeration by incorporating porous scoria or pumice in the mix and remedy nutrition depletion with moderate fertilization.

It's easy to forget the power of soil, since most of its action is hidden. Addressing soil reveals the workings of water, chemistry, physics, and biology, drawing us closer to knowing a soil that 'just feels right'. A little effort invested early will pay back in the years of pleasure you'll find in your floriferous crevice garden.

There are many ingredients for soil mixes but most are made of only two or three ingredients and often coarse sand alone is used.

Ingredients for a soil mix or medium

The different components of a mix will interact with one another in complex ways, but each usually has some fundamental strength to warrant its use, and certain weaknesses to be mindful of in the context of growing plants.

Gravels

Gravel is just small rocks of different sizes. Gravel mixed into the soil will offer nutritional properties of its parent material; more is available for instance from soft sedimentary stone, and little from hard volcanic or metamorphic ones. Most purchased gravels will have a certain amount of fines, or dust, which can act as fertilizer and lend more available mineral nutrition (see below). Rounded river gravels are least useful and also roll around on the soil surface. The particles of sharp gravels brace against one another better, create more air spaces and are a more stable surface dressing.

Mixing gravel into the soil does not necessarily improve its ability to drain; it makes the soil effectively drier only by displacing other materials that hold water, and this actually slows percolation and absorption. This is not directly useful for a plant, except perhaps to force it to grow deeper roots.

Gravel to be used in the soil should not exceed screen sizes of 0.5–1cm (¼–½in), or it will prevent even narrow-headed shovels from penetrating. While it can be used to stop or slow spill-out of a mix from cracks and crevices in steep walls, the best use of gravel remains as top-dressing to reduce surface evaporation and splashing of the soil from rain or watering.

Fines

Fines make up the dust that is intentionally screened out of gravel. They often add mineral nutrition and can retain moisture, and fill otherwise open voids between larger-particle materials, which is useful or not depending on what you seek. Gravel fines can be a valuable, predictable source of silt when you need that particular texture. In drier and continental climates, some gardeners are finding that gravel fines (especially decomposed granite) alone work for them as a one-ingredient rock garden soil in the same way that sand works universally for gardeners in wetter climates. Limestone fines seem particularly prone to 'setting' like concrete, which is not surprising, as they are a key component of Portland cement. Let a sample of your fines settle in a glass jar to find out which type and in what ratio they are. In a sand-based or coarser mix, fines should not exceed 10 percent of the overall volume of a mix to ensure ample pores for air and water remain.

Scoria and pumice

Both scoria and pumice are forms of lava and feature air pockets, making them very lightweight conveyors of porosity and drainage in the rock garden; in fact, pumice is so light it floats in water and this quality makes it useful in containers that need to be moved. Scoria is often a main ingredient in cactus mixes and is said to lend acidity. Pumice can look and feel just like perlite, but is expected to last a lot longer. Large stones of either can be used in the garden, much like tufa, but when used in a soil mix seek out 1cm (½in) in size or smaller. The finest screenings will contain dust that will act like sand, often needing little else to work alone as a brilliant soil mix for containers. Lava stones vary in availability by region but can sometimes be sourced by intercepting the supply to brick and cinder block factories. They also vary in chemical makeup, neither tending to be especially rich with their own nutrition. To find your local source, make friends with bonsai and orchid growers, who are well aware of these exotic commodities.

Sand

Sourced from beaches and river bottoms, or screened from crushing gravel, sand varies tremendously in particle size and shape, depending on material and age. It is distinguished from sandy soils, whose sand particles are usually magnitudes smaller. For the crevice garden, use what is called a 'sharp' sand, which varies little in size, or the smaller grains will lock in between the larger ones and block those precious pores. Names vary, but 'construction', or 'concrete' sand is usually very coarse and works well as a main ingredient for a free-draining mix while 'masonry' sand may have fines, which may or may not be desirable to you. Dark, gray, and dirty-colored sand, derived from a variety of eroding rocks (and revealing a mix of particle colors under magnification), are more apt to have available minerals for rock-loving plants. Pale, light-colored sands are usually the least nutritious, supplying little more plant food than broken glass.

Composts

Composts are made of pure organic material that both supplies and stores nutrients. The last stage of full organic decomposition is 'humus', referred to as the life-force of the soil. It holds onto nutrients and water, like clay, but also adds air and promotes drainage. A benefit to rock gardeners, well-decomposed humus delivers nutrients at a slower and more even rate. Even in the richest part of the rock garden with the hungriest plants, compost is usually no more than 20 percent of your soil volume. Any humus in your soil mix must be well decomposed, or else massive and unwanted settling may result over time as the organic material continues to decompose to virtually no volume. Natural rocky soils are considered high in organics when they contain more than 1 percent. In a garden, 5 percent would be on the high end for a crevice – or, one part compost to nineteen parts everything else!

Manufactured materials

Expanded shale and other permeable aggregates look like gravel, but their individual particles hold water and nutrients within them, while the large air spaces in between them can be preserved for powerful, permanent aeration. Expanded shale is the most common, used as the main ingredient in green roof soil mixes and hydroponics, and to add strength to structural concrete.

Calcined clays include Turface in the USA (the red covering on the baseball field) or Seramis clay granules, marketed in Europe for growing plants. These are more or less interchangeable, and most have been fired in an industrial kiln to harden them. Crushed flower pots are also a permeable aggregate and have been listed in soil mixes for at least a hundred years (and are well known by bonsai growers).

All aggregates supply the soil trinity: water, air, and nutrients. Their porosity holds water like a sponge, drawing it away from the gaps between the particles because of their capillarity, leaving the gaps to hold air, while the hardness of the particles keeps them from eroding and collapsing on the air spaces. This also makes them permanent in the garden and reusable in pots. If a particular permeable aggregate has a lot of dust (particles finer than 3mm (1/8in), it might be useful to screen it out so it doesn't occupy those precious air spaces, especially in pots.

This odd class of permeable aggregate materials varies in chemistry, but most test out with high cation exchange capacity, or nutrient availability, especially if they are derived in some way from clay. In this way, they hold nutrients without the need for organic material in the soil mix. Hydroponic growers, orchid growers, and even rock gardeners have successfully grown difficult plants in pure permeable aggregate.

The Swedish gardener and force of nature Peter Korn replaced the soil in his entire garden with pure sand, with glorious horticultural results. As it turns out, sand is the perfect way to manage the garden moisture in his climate in Gothenburg, Sweden, and he is able to achieve different results by varying its depth.

Soil recipes for gardens

Here are some soil mixes, gathered from both friends and traditions, that we've named and described to inform a new crevice gardener or enrich a seasoned one. The goal is to make something you don't already have in the garden, which complements it by satisfying needs it cannot. Your local climate and watering regime will dictate which medium works for you. Extremely well-drained soils work well in wet gardens, but are too dry for unirrigated desert gardens. But even the desert can be too wet – a single heavy rain on heavy clay can rot the plants dwelling there.

Don't forget the difference between plants which love organic matter versus the group which has crept to the tops of mountains to avoid it! There is a wide range in between, too. Err on the side of a more open soil with fewer nutrients, because organics and fines can be added to a garden but not subtracted. There is also no sense in over-engineering a soil since every ingredient affects every factor, and at some point too many additives bring diminishing returns. Unless you are building your garden to grow a predetermined genus, the best is to aim for a one-size-fits-all soil that will grow the majority of genera, and modify that as needed.

The Traditionalist

The Traditionalist will grow a wide range of easy alpines such as *Erigeron scopulinus*.

- *1 part gravel, roughly 3mm (1/8in) size*
- *1 part compost*
- *1 part existing soil*

This classic is easy to source. The gravel provides drainage by displacement but doesn't necessarily oxygenate the soil. A true soil guarantees nutrients and water retention, and the compost provides additional nutrients which will feed floriferous, herbaceous rock garden plants. However, it will settle over time and may oust plants that love mineral soils. This is a good choice for a larger garden with more soil surface than rocks, since a third of the ingredients are in place, but not ideal for a crevice garden built for chasmophytes.

The Korn Mix

- *1 part pure sand*

Choose your sand well. Much air and water can pass through, and the surface will need to be protected by gravel so it does not wash or blow away. It is too dry for most plants in a dry climate garden, but just right in a wetter climate – adjust the depth to suit the need. Hungry plants will starve, ruderal plants will thrive, and the humans will find it easy to weed, dig, and play in.

The Rooftop Mix

- *1 part expanded shale or similar*
- *1 part compost*

Full of air and full of nutrients and of little weight, this is an aerated mix good for containers and green roofs growing leafy, hungry plants. It will need regular water in dry climates.

The Steppe Garden Mix

- *2 parts sand*
- *2 parts expanded shale or similar*
- *1 part compost*

Used at Denver Botanic Gardens, and inspired by green roof mixes, this has proved versatile in hosting a wide variety of plants.

The Haenni

- *2 parts sand*
- *2 parts scoria*
- *1 part compost*

This mix works brilliantly in an irrigated or moist garden, creating a zone of loose root space which will stay open for decades with the scoria providing backup air, water, and nutrient reserves. Adapted from a mix used by our friend Rod Haenni of Denver.

Desert Rat

- *2 parts sandy loam, silt, or gravel fines*
- *3 parts coarse sand*
- *1 part (optional) expanded shale or similar*

Useful in a dry garden in a dry climate, this employs the permanent looseness of sand but with the nutrient and water storage of the others. Your native desert plants will thrive and celebrate the nearly zero organics. Gravel fines often form a sort of crust, keeping the mix from eroding if exposed.

The Steppe Garden Mix is used around the rock features at Denver Botanic Gardens.

The Sellars: On The Rocks

· *6 parts coarse sand*
· *1 part crusher fines*

Our friend David Sellars in British Columbia uses this for most rock garden plants, adding a bit of compost for those that want it. He says it 'suits saxifrages, high-altitude alpines and dryland plants such as *Eriogonum*'. The sand providing excellent drainage dominates, while the fines provide mineral nutrients and some water retention.

The lovely *Lewisiopsis tweedyi* living it up on a diet of The Sellars: On The Rocks.

A Balanced Marriage

· *4 parts sand*
· *2 parts expanded shale or similar*
· *1 part or less, optional compost*

This is a good crevice garden mix to use within an existing garden. Compost can be added to pockets for the hungry plants. Sand drains water wildly while expanded shale keeps a sane bank account balance of nutrients and water. This mix works in all climates, but requires regular irrigation in the driest places.

Home-Baked

· *Sterilized and screened local soil*

True soils going into tight crevices or seedling mixes can be sterilized through whatever zany method you can think of, such as stock pots, pressure cookers, and microwaves. Most gardeners end up cooking it somehow so they can have the fertile humates and texture of their beloved garden soil without the potential diseases and bugs.

Soil for containers

A pot must provide the same benefits as the earth, if not more, and in a limited space. Lacking the sharing of moisture, nutrients, and air that happens in the depth of the earth, all of these resources must be supplied in a pot, so container and soilless mixes must be richer to compensate.

Commenting on *Phalaenopsis* orchids being beautifully grown in styrofoam packing peanuts, Denver horticulturist Jim Borland once said, 'You can grow a plant in anything, but you have to water it right.' The inverse also applies, of course, so you can tailor a mix to your climate and watering style. A heavy mix must be watered infrequently and carefully so as to avoid drowning, maybe even suited to a greenhouse where it's protected from rain, while an open mix can be watered liberally but might need to be watched more closely to avoid a fatal drying out.

The soil is serious business for the plant in a pot, because it is a prisoner and has no place to escape. We invent mixes that work for our lives, our budgets, our space, and our plants. When it comes to water retention and nutrients, we must choose ingredients that strike a balance between too much and too little. The proportions of materials used in a mix will affect its drainage, but their effect is not linear, since different materials interact with one another to change the overall behavior of the mix.

Generally, the larger the trough or container, the more like garden soil it can be and the more stable it will be to temperature, moisture, and nutrition changes. For such long-term service, just a handful of garden dirt thrown in can help supply minerals and micronutrients easily that are absent from commercial mixes and raw materials.

There is such a thing as too much aeration. If there is an overabundance of large particles like gravel, clods of finer materials in between do not touch. These no longer drain from capillarity and water cannot seep upward from below. The mix only drains through the large pores which dominate, and there is little storage for water and nutrients. This effect could happen within a potting mix dominated by gravel, perlite, or scoria. After seeing how often your container needs water, you'll hone in on the perfect, reliable stand-by to start with and adjust for future containers in your climate. See soil recipes for containers on page 147.

Be sure to group plants with similar needs together such as xeric combinations like *Penstemon rupicola* and *Anthemis cretica*, top, and *Acantholimon venustum* in front of *Verbascum* x 'Letitia', left. Bonus points if they bloom at the same time.

Plants in the design

Generally speaking, the bigger the rocks in a crevice garden, the bigger the allowable plants. Rock gardening culture suggests a 30cm (12in) maximum height rule, with most smaller, jewel-box crevice plants capped at 15cm (6in). Since a primary concern in crevice gardening is to accommodate special plants, they have a high priority in the design.

By default, the crevice garden lends itself to diversity. If you are a mad collector of the choice, rare, and eccentric, you may not care about the garden's overall aesthetic, because the stone backdrop, as well as common forms such as buns, cushions, carpets, and tufts, can create a certain visual harmony in even the most mixed crevice planting. After all, both the monoculture and the plant zoo happen in nature.

For high naturalism, use multiples of each plant so that when they all bloom together, a natural drift is created across the garden. The same can be achieved by carefully managing self-sown seedlings. Knowing the colors and bloom periods of your plants will also help you to get the most out of your plant design, and the experienced gardener will coordinate color combinations and timings that complement one another. Just like rock placement, uneven spacing between the plants and uneven shaped groupings will maximize natural effect.

Consider the ratio of visible plants to visible rocks; the stones can't warm and dry the garden as well if they are completely covered. In this regard, a little plant pruning or removal can go a long way. On the flip side, a few big plants, or even just one, can help a crevice garden to appear older and related to the surrounding landscape.

Choose small plants that are to scale with the size of your garden.

Aggressively rhizomatous species will need to be sited where rocks are large enough to prevent their roots from growing below or around the stones. Also be cognizant of where you plant thorny or toxic plants such as cacti and spurges. Lastly, don't locate plants that you may want to divide, like bulbs, in a paper-thin crack, and be aware that taller herbaceous plants may potentially shadow slow-growing cushions when you're not looking!

In the end, your plants are the element of the crevice garden that most expresses your personal preferences. Respect your own tastes and allow yourself to focus on what makes you happiest.

Consider the plant to rock ratio. Do you want to see the rocks or are you happy if they become completely covered with plants?

BUILDING A CREVICE GARDEN IN 8 STEPS

Certain sites and gardens may require the steps of construction to be in a different order, such as finishing one side first because of access limitations, or starting with the buried rocks first in a diagonal build, but this chapter follows the most common experience: from the ground up. It helps to revisit your design, however vague, and be reminded of key principles as you build, because the most critical design decisions are made not with a pencil, but with a rock in hand.

It's daunting when the stone is in play but, with a little planning, this can be by far the most exciting time.

CARDINAL RULES

for a happy, natural-looking crevice garden

Do

- Aim for narrow crevices, averaging approximately 2.5cm (1in) wide.
- Keep light mediums (sandy) above heavy soils (clays).
- Use an irregularly shaped footprint.
- Orient rock strata oblique to other nearby lines.
- Build tall for drama and drainage.
- Use asymmetry.
- Use all sizes of rock.
- Bury rocks deeply – at least by half.
- Plant multiples of at least some plants.

Don't

- Choose oversized plants.
- Space stones widely so they don't touch or offer much to plants.
- Bury rocks shallowly so they are unstable if stepped on.
- Use too much compost.

Avoid

- Building under trees.
- Siting garden adjacent to weedy rhizomatous plants.
- Using multiple types of rock.
- Planting sharp or toxic plants close to paths.
- Pinching your fingers.

Construction terms

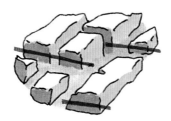

Stratum

A line of orientation across the crevice garden.

Secondary strata

A subordinate, weaker pattern in the stones.

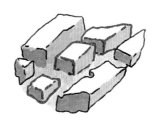

Course

The rocks within one stratum.

Faces of layers

The two parallel sides of the rock which are orientated as strata and may be buried or exposed.

Side walls

Faces of layers which are exposed.

Faces of edges

The 'rim' of a rock that faces upward.

Faces of ends

The edge of the rock that faces outward or is buried against another.

Vertical joint

Where the faces of two rocks in a course meet.

Return

Where rocks that edge the garden enter the ground.

It's time to commit and simply start building. From assembling all the materials onsite in an organized manner (staging) to the final product, it helps to have a plan or system to help the project flow smoothly. Using common sense, you might find that building is easier than you think!

Step 1:
Source and stage materials

To find good crevice garden rock, check with quarries, construction companies, landscapers, and gravel companies. You can also use roadside stone, but be sure you have permission to collect it. Local landscape suppliers often have rocks cleaned and stacked on pallets for easier transport and storage, but they are often more expensive.

Ideally, you'll hand-pick the stone from a quarry, which allows you to choose only the best stone and minimizes unusable rock. However, some quarries won't allow hand-picking; they will simply scoop a pile of rock into a dump truck, which automatically gives you the variety of sizes you need. This is usually the cheapest way to get stone, but it will probably include some dirt and unusable pieces. You can break those waste stones with a sledgehammer into chips and top-dressing if the rock is soft enough and newly chipped fragments match the look you want. This may be your only top-dressing if there is no gravel available to match your stone.

Aim for stones that will feel big in the space you have but can still be moved with relative ease. Don't under- or overestimate your strength! The majority should be the most comfortable size for you to handle by hand, but also get some that will be hard to move, perhaps requiring equipment or help, and plenty of stones that are smaller as well. Variety is key.

For taking your purchase home, the smallest full-size pickup carries one-half ton of rock. A normal dump truck carries 10–12 tons, while a long dump truck carries up to 20. Do some math and you'll usually find that it's more economical to hire a big truck than make dozens of trips in your car. Of course in many places, hand picking the stone from a quarry is not an option, in which case you'll have to get the materials delivered, which is when proper estimates are more important.

Clockwise from top left: Quarry-sourced stone offers the best selection. Dollies (hand carts) are healthier for carting large pieces. A pickup truck is useful for hauling large consignments of rock. Palletized stone is convenient but may lack variety of size.

Estimating rock

Estimating rock tonnage in three dimensions is approximate. There are a handful of reasons why it is unavoidably approximate. First, the very nature of a crevice garden is that rocks are buried deeply with just their small faces above ground. Second, how tightly the rocks are set together; if your build favors narrow crevices, it will consume more stone. Third, how deeply each of the stones are buried will vastly affect the total amount needed. Imagine a stone is roughly the shape of a domino brick; it will literally cover half the surface area if buried with the narrowest end exposed versus one of its long narrow sides. In taller constructions, it becomes more important to bury rocks deeper like this to stabilize them and support their neighbors, so the effect of needing more rock for a taller garden is compounded. Similarly, a crevice garden with a rough or undulating surface will usually use more stone than one with a smooth, consolidated surface. In general, it's always better to source more than you think you'll need. Working in US tons, a tiny 1 x 1m (3 x 3ft) pocket garden can use one half-ton of sandstone or one ton of granite, while a garden the size of a big dining-room table, 2 x 2m (6 x 6ft), can be two to five tons. An installation the size of a small car – 3 x 3m (10 x 10ft) – easily uses nine tons.

Rock weight also varies by stone type due to their different densities, and each kind of stone, especially limestone, can vary. The variation is usually not more than 20%, say between a granite and a sandstone, but the heaviest gabbro can be almost 50% heavier than a very light sandstone. Tufa, pumice, and scoria are rarely available, can vary significantly, and are in a class all their own in terms of weight. One way to accurately calculate tonnage for a large new project is to build a small part of the garden with a known amount of material and work out what you'll need to finish the job.

Roughly calculating how much rock you will need

The simplest method to calculate how much rock you need is based on the footprint of your proposed garden – its square footage in two dimensions.

Then, you need to estimate the depth of the rock over that square footage. Optionally, for better accuracy and for larger projects, you must consider how a bulging surface has more square footage – like a dome versus a flat circle – so you will increase that surface-area estimate accordingly. But in most instances, this is where we estimate the approximate average depth of stone across the garden - this gives us the third dimension to multiply by for an approximate volume.

Next, this volume must be reduced by the prevalence of stone versus open crevice, and a good rule of thumb is about ⅔ rock, leaving ⅓ of surface being composed of the crevices between the rocks.

Of course stone is generally sold by weight, not volume, so the last part of the calculation is to convert the volume measurement into lb or kg. Not all rocks are the same density, as noted above. Thus to figure out the weight of rock you need, multiply your final volume estimate by the density of rock. That will give you about as accurate an estimate as possible.

Estimating mediums

Calculating soil media is a little easier. You will find the volume of media by simply measuring the three dimensions of a shape within a shell of rock. That is, a shape whose length and width are within the inside of your outside rocks and whose height is one rock's depth shorter than the proposed height of the garden. That shape can be a cube within your mound, or even a cone or dome if those better represent the general shape of your garden. The shortage in this estimation for media that will fill the actual crevices is usually perfectly offset by the subsoil that is generated when digging for your first stones which are buried in the ground itself.

Formulae for volume assume construction is on flat ground; sloping or uneven terrain usually requires considerably less material because it has its own built-in topography. Again, build in stages to get a good idea of what you'll eventually need. If you end up with too much soil, it can always be worked into a lawn or used to top up adjacent garden beds. Sometimes soil medium is sold by weight – the salesperson should have a guide to help you convert if needed. For example, 0.8 cubic meters of sand (1yd³) can weigh more than 1.45 tonnes (1.6 US tons) when wet! That won't come home in the trunk of the car.

Estimating top-dressing

Top-dressing only needs to be roughly 1.25–2.5cm (½–1in) thick and is needed just to cover the soil between the crevices and any open-soil skirts or pockets – a little goes a long way. There are several ways to estimate how much you need. The basic key is to guess by appearance what percentage of surface area is crevice and not solid rock – for most crevice gardens it will be 10–33 per cent. So you'll simply multiply your surface area by 0.1–0.33 to find crevice surface area.

Most builders just eyeball what they need and bring it by the bucket because even a large garden will require only small amounts. Bagged materials have the advantage of being hand-carried and stored easily, but if you need a truckload, it's to best buy in bulk. Don't forget to match your garden's rock and avoid uniform gravel size.

Because rocks and other materials are natural, irregular things, and your garden is highly variable itself, there is no perfect calculation. If you must be as precise as possible, use several estimation strategies and compare them – the average is usually remarkably accurate.

Staging

First, take note of your access limits. How wide are your garden gates relative to wheelbarrows, hand carts, rock carts, or heavy equipment? Find a place to accept deliveries and store materials until they are used. Avoid dumping rock or gravel on nice paving, as falling rock will score big holes in it, and use plywood, tarp or old carpets to prevent soil or gravel piles from spoiling turf. Paving that will see a lot of truck traffic can be protected with plywood or even a temporary pile of dirt or sand.

Soil mixes bound for a new garden should be stockpiled so you can add to areas that settle or require revision. You may have a supplier mix your soil for you, or you can do it yourself on a tarp, in a wheelbarrow, in a bucket, or on-site. Small batches can be produced in small hand cement-mixers. A beautiful pile of new soil mix might need covering to protect it from weed seed in long-term storage.

The stone may require several moves to stockpile it on-site, which is the perfect opportunity to get acquainted with it. Lay it all out and organize it by shape and size to identify any fun fossils or pretty colors you'll want to highlight in the construction. When you stage rock, make sure to leave yourself room immediately around the garden and paths for walking and wheelbarrows.

How much rock?

Start with a calculation of area:
1.82m x 1.82m = 3.31 m²
(6ft x 6ft = 36 ft²)

If the average stone is 30cm (1ft) deep, then our garden's volume is
$3.31m^2$ x .3m = $0.993m^3$ ($1m^3$)
($36ft^2$ x 1ft = $36ft^3$)

Now, account for the crevices, which cover about a third of the surface
$1m^3$ x 2/3 = $0.67m^3$
($36ft^3$ x 2/3 = $24ft^3$)

For weight, we'll use the density of granite, which is $2691kg/m^3$ or $168lb/ft^3$
$0.67m^3$ x 2691(kg/m^3) = 180kg
($24ft^3$ x 168[lb/ft^3] = 4032lb = 2 US tons)

How much soil medium?

A cone is a great approximation of the shape of a crevice garden and it's also the general shape of an actual pile of sand or media.

First understand how to work out the volume of a cone:
$V = 1/3 \, h \, \pi \, r^2$ (and for us, a radius is 1/2 the width of a garden)

Then apply this to your garden:
Volume = 1/3 x height x π x (1/2 width)²

Example 1
A typical backyard crevice garden 3m (10ft) wide whose media is piled 1m (3ft) tall:
1/3 x 1m x π x (1/2 x 3m)² = $2.4m^3$
1/3 x 3ft x π x (1/2 x 10ft)² = $78.5ft^3$ = $2.9yd^3$
This garden will need about $2.4m^3$ (roughly $3yd^3$), about three loads in a heavy-duty pickup.

Example 2
A small crevice garden with a footprint 1m (3ft) wide and media piled .3m (1ft) tall:
1/3 x .3 x π x (1/2 x 1)² = $0.079m^3$
1/3 x 1 x π x (1/2 x 3)² = $2.36ft^3$
A tiny garden's $.079m^3$ ($2.36ft^3$) of soil medium is a little more than a hand-held bag of media and almost fills a small wheelbarrow.

Example 3
A larger 6m (20ft) wide crevice garden 1m (3.5ft) high:
1/3 x 1 x π x (1/2 x 6)² = $9.42m^3$
1/3 x 3.5 x π x (1/2 x 20)² = $366ft^3$ = $13.6yd^3$
The big garden needs $9.42m^3$ ($13.6yd^3$), which is about one regular dump truck (or tipper in the UK).

Note
π = 3.14

How much top-dressing?

To determine an amount of top-dressing, start by calculating the surface area, either flat for a rough number or the three-dimensional surface for a more accurate number. Multiply this by the percentage of the area which is not already covered in stones. We'll assume 33% = 0.33 here. Lastly, multiply the resulting area by its depth in the same unit.

Example
To cover a third of an area that is $9.3m^2$ ($100ft^2$) to a depth of 2.5cm (1in) in gravel:
$9.3m^2$ x 0.33 x 0.025m = $.077m^3$
($100ft^2$ x 0.33 x 0.0833ft = $2.74ft^3$)

Notes
2.5cm = .025m and 1in = .0833ft

Divide cubic feet by 27 if you need cubic yards. In our example, the volume of gravel is so small it would fill roughly two 12-litre buckets (just four 5-gallon buckets)!

Step 2:
Mark and cut the footprint

The creative process begins with marking the footprint on the ground, using hoses, ropes, string, spray paint, pegs, or even baking flour. Again, think natural and asymmetrical. Vary the lengths of any lines and the size of any contained shapes.

After the footprint has been established, use a shovel to dig out the edges of the perimeter. Dig deeply enough that your perimeter stones, when laid in this trench, will be 'planted' at least half their size below ground level. The perimeter rocks provide critical structural support for a great deal of lateral weight.

The average sod will die if buried at least 30cm (12in). Otherwise, completely clean out strongly rhizomatous grasses or you'll be fighting zombies of lawn past. Weed seeds will not be a problem buried under a rock garden, but roots and rhizomes of weeds will be disastrous. Taking extra months to eradicate these ahead of time is worth the trouble compared to years and years of fighting them afterwards.

It's amazing how much dirt you generate just digging the perimeter. The spoil will start to create a mound in the middle of your future garden – be sure to break it up a bit so that air pockets don't contribute to settling. Already you'll see your crevice garden beginning to take shape.

Dig out the edges and mound existing soil after stripping the turf.

Above: Place new soil over existing mounded soil.
Left: Mounded and sculpted soil shows the
garden taking form with multiple high points of
differing stature.

The height of the final
crevice garden will be
'one rock' taller than the
mounded media; set a few
rocks, if only temporarily,
to picture this.

Step 3:
Mound medium in the middle

Next, add the bulk of the new soil mix in a mound. If you encounter a lot of earthworms or perennial weed roots, lay down a geotextile barrier on top of your native soil (and the disturbed mound of it in the middle) before the mix goes on top. Work smart. Give yourself easy wheelbarrow access, favoring more small loads. If a sandy medium is difficult to drive on with a wheelbarrow, or there are obstacles in your way, use stones or wooden planks to temporarily 'pave' this path; the ease pays off.

Sculpting your mound of medium is the critical step in forming your dramatic rock outcrop. Your stone will essentially sit on top of this layer, so create a form a stone's depth short of the height you seek. You can even place a few stones or draw lines on it at this stage to give you a clearer idea as to the final height and orientation. Be creative, courageous, and bold! It's easier to move a loose soil mix like you're playing in a sandbox than to move it with rocks on top. Asymmetry is key; the best crevice gardens are a nice mixture of irregular peaks, valleys, ridges, and slopes. Sculpt the pile so that it has one point higher than all the others, and put it anywhere but the exact center. Multiple points are great but be sure that they differ in height.

Mounded soil furrowed with a shovel gives a good indication of what your crevice garden will look like even before a single rock is placed.

Step 4:
Set first and perimeter stones

Placing the first stone can be daunting, even with all the preparation and thought beforehand. It's a big deal because it informs all the other rocks that follow it. Sometimes we have a toast to celebrate the first rock.

Top row: Address the steep, tricky bits first with deeply planted rock. Contain the media with supportive perimeter stones.
Bottom row: Take a compass bearing of these to ensure they are oriented in strata. Rock bars and other simple tools make the heaviest rock easier.

All edge stones must return to ground level in a natural way that implies a larger outcrop underneath.

Staggered side wall stones support one another, exposing the faces of edges and layers, creating stability and a natural effect.

Start with the large rocks first, perhaps as perimeters for the footprint or to deal with the steepest or most visible parts of the outcrop. After you decide you are happy with the first stone, take a compass bearing on the magnetic orientation of its dominant flat side – from zero to 359 degrees – and let that guide the rest of your garden. It's always hard when staring at a blank page, but after the first stones, it becomes easier.

If the largest rocks are up high, they'll need soil mix to support them. If they are placed where future rocks will support them, you can use temporary blocks or stakes to shore them until they are stabilized by their neighbors – this is especially true in diagonal construction. Extreme diagonal or horizontal construction is easier if you start with the rocks on the bottom – those leaned upon – whether they are the largest or not. Diagonal builds are tricky, too, because those first stones will have both 'dip and strike' (tilt and orientation) to follow.

Choose the nicest parts of the rocks for exposed faces and pleasing returns to ground level, keeping the overall form in mind. Again, avoid symmetry in the spacing between rocks, the visible size of each, and the height of their tops. Imagine the outcrop as one large rock weathered over time into hundreds of pieces, each complementing the next. Steeper slopes and aspects will need more support from big, deep rocks below.

Rock bars are about 2m (6ft) long and give you supreme leverage so that a single person can scoot a stone weighing up to 400kg (900lb). You can use a small nearby stone or piece of wood as a fulcrum against the medium so the bar doesn't sink into it. Keep in mind that your metal rock bar and shovels will interfere with the needle of the compass if it is nearby!

Check the majority of your first rocks with a compass, especially if you are setting them at some distance from each other. Misorientation will reveal itself when the rockwork meets in the middle. Keep in mind that faces of edges are better at creating large, steep, stable aspects than side walls; they also add nice crevices to those steep slopes.

Perimeter stones that expose the ends of courses must naturally return to grade without overhang. The remaining perimeter stones will tend to be side walls: just bury the stone by at least half and stand it vertically. You might weep at burying 90 percent of a lovely stone, but perimeter side walls provide critical support, and it's very common that they give out if not buried deeply enough. They can also be shored up with other stones from the outside, like a buttress, or by buried stones inside. The larger a side wall, the more support it needs.

As each course returns to grade or side walls overlap, be sure to offset the perimeter stones so the faces of edges follow the curve of the footprint of the garden. Vary their size as well so that you don't end up with a uniform pearl necklace effect. Select for any tilt, angles, unevenness, or character so that the superior face is outward. If you need to, leave out a few perimeter stones for wheelbarrow access to the middle of your mound, or make a temporary ramp to overcome a steep lip you have built.

At this point, work the soil mix around the bases of your perimeter and large stones, trying to collapse air pockets while it's easy. Sandy mixes can be rammed without worry of compaction. Use the handle end of a shovel, your boots, or other tools of your invention. Subtle adjustments to the height of your large stones are more easily done at this stage, by digging soil out from under them, prying them up and backfilling from below, or even ramming soil underneath in a hydraulic effect that easily and gently increases their height. Very steep slopes may not sustain themselves when they are merely soil, so build those sections first.

Step 5:
Lay rock courses across

Courses are like ribs on a torso, running the whole width or length of the garden and connecting big stones to the perimeter like a frame. They are the essential next step for sedimentary stone, but not critical with metamorphic and more irregular stone, which can be worked in patches around larger stones or starting up from the perimeter. In diagonal construction, you may be forced to start on one side of the garden (the stones on which the rest lean) and work to the other side. You may also have to do this if access to the garden is limited, like painting a floor starting in the farthest corner and finishing at the door. If this is your workflow, ration the size and quality of rock so you don't use all the good stuff on one side and leave yourself with nothing but boring rocks on the other. Don't worry – your garden needs boring rocks to support the pretty ones, which in turn are all background to pretty plants. That's why setting a few complete courses across the garden is often best, forcing you to work all over the garden at once, so that as your varying moods and styles occur, they are not sequestered in corners but spread uniformly throughout.

Make an effort to keep courses the same thickness along their whole length, emulating nature. Sorting the stone into similar widths prior to construction helps, though try to mix lengths so that members of a course don't look like bricks. Let the stones rise up and down, avoiding perfect levelness, and select for their most interesting faces.

Orchestrating how the most visible rocks relate to each other is the great secret to arranging stone. In nature, the forces that broke off an outcrop's exposed edge would also apply to other stones nearby. In the garden, well-unified stones look as though they were once the same stone and have just a crack separating them.

Lay the courses.

The bones, or largest rocks, make up the structural form of the outcrop.

Once you get to this point you're roughly halfway through the build.

Top: A long broad slab is a striking feature which serves both aesthetic and structural purposes.
Above: Here, the slabby side wall retains the soil in the next crevice and serves as a retaining wall for the next step up in height.
Right: The high notes of the design are the exposed side walls or cliffs.

It's wise to finish one course at a time, from one edge of the footprint to the opposite, then move on to another course elsewhere in the crevice garden. Check your courses with a compass – some builders use a string line or wooden planks to stay oriented. You may have to use temporary props for tall, skinny stones that don't want to stand on their own before being supported by surrounding rock and soil.

Stay hydrated, caffeinated, or whatever makes you happy, but be sure to take breaks, even spacing out your work over days or weeks if possible. Viewing the ongoing construction with fresh eyes helps you to see clearly how it is shaping up. Be fearless about pulling rocks out and resetting them. There is no law against changing your mind: no one is watching, and it's your garden. Most folks redo a corner of their crevice garden or add onto it within a year. Your garden is alive and evolving now!

More courses

After you're locked in a frame or pattern with a few courses, it's time to fill the garden in. The cardinal direction is already set, so each course parallels the next, lying laterally, conforming to the contours and slopes of your soil mound. Now you can work more freely around the garden; we suggest starting in the most prominent or structurally dramatic or challenging areas, where you might need a better selection of bigger stones. Leave flatter, gentler areas for last, where stability and prominence are not an issue.

The main consideration when laying a course next to another is to ensure you step it up or down or stay level with adjacent contour. Vary the height so that some steps change just an inch or so, while others are much higher, emulating exposed cliff faces. Here is where you have the opportunity to bury ugly sides of stones while exposing others, deeply overlapping stone courses to allow for steep yet stable slopes.

Vertical joints

A vertical joint is where the ends of two rocks in a course meet. Generally, vertical joints are staggered for stability, in much the way bricks overlap. This is relatively easy with a variety of stones. Staggering joints is especially important when stepping down from a course; the new course below must support that above by being tall enough, at least at that joint, not only to hide it but to provide support to the outside of both ends of the meeting stones, like a buttress. If unsupported, the loose ends of stones can eventually splay open, resulting in soil spilling from the crevice. Generally, at least half the outside of a stone must be buried or connected to another rock to stay upright; you'll get a sense of this quickly while hunched on your knee pads, jiggling adjacent stones to see when they are stable.

There are times to break the rule about overlap, too. This follows a certain intuition that whatever force of nature put a crack through a course also went through adjacent layers. Offset them just slightly so the crack is not a perfect crossroad, or at least not through too many courses. You can better achieve this when the stones are well buried and the courses aren't making huge steps between them. Hide vertical joints if they don't look natural to you.

Take plenty of breaks at this stage, looking at the overall garden. A bottle of beer or a cup of tea is the perfect amount of time to step away and return to your work with fresh eyes.

Secondary faces

A great way to make a jagged crevice garden look cohesive is to orient a second face (the first being the main strata) to another plane that is common in the stone. This happens in nature as a result of secondary geologic cleavage, which leaves repeated planes all over the landscape, letting you know they are made of the same stuff. Pro tip: don't align secondary planes quite as strictly as the first (which is usually the strata). You'll earn your black belt in rock-arranging by adding a third plane, but again, not as strictly as the first two.

Repeated complementary angles are the most aesthetically pleasing.

Step 6:
Set the rest of the stone

Once the large rocks and a few complete courses are in place, you can generally approximate the orientation of smaller rocks. Set the rest of your stones on top of the contours of the original sculpted soil pile, digging the rocks into it or adding soil as needed. Again, ration yourself for size and quality of rock to prevent consolidation of one kind in an area, and don't use all your nicest rocks first! You will find that, overall, placing the first stones is slow going, mid-process stonework is steady, and the last stones can be situated quickly. At the Cheyenne Botanic Gardens, the first, massive stone took 45 minutes to place, but a few weeks later, softball-sized stones each took mere seconds.

Cover more surface area with longer, less deeply buried rocks. Sometimes, these can be so shallow they are just veneers that function above ground as a crevice. Take flat, easy areas as an opportunity to hide ugly rocks, using their smallest and best face. Still, bury half the stones' mass as a rule – your plants' roots will appreciate it. When you are down to the last stone in an area, seek out a rock that works as a wedge. This will apply a little pressure to adjacent stones, keeping them tight and less apt to wander side-to-side in the coming years.

Below: Pack the crevices to eliminate air pockets and stabilize stones.

Right: Add smaller rocks by feel once larger rocks are in place.

It's smoother work when you start low and work up, since higher rocks are all nestling into lower ones. Store your in-transit rocks above you on the mound so you can easily pull them downhill while you set them. When transporting the stream of stone to the garden, don't forget to use your wheels – rock carts, small furniture carts, and wheelbarrows – and beware of slapping rocks down very fast (however satisfying). Stop and assess your work to make sure you're adding variations in form, if only subtly.

Don't rely on soil to support your rocks anywhere but below them, especially in freezing climates. Frost heave will move rocks so fast you'll feel that geologic time sped up to smite you. If you have a side wall that wants to collapse on a crevice below (which is true of every single course in diagonal construction), use rocks like a strut, wide enough to brace a gap but not long enough to occupy the whole crevice. Strut and brace stones can even be buried or hidden if their outside faces don't fit in. When in doubt, wiggle your stones to see how stable they are. Most should not move much when you walk on them before the crevices are filled with soil, and none of them should move once construction is complete.

Good plants hide bad rockwork!

Our friend Jeremy Schmidt, grounds and research supervisor at Juniper Level Botanic Gardens, says you can use 'horticultural duct-tape' (i.e. plants) to hide unsatisfying rock work if something bugs you, and you can't find the right rock to fix it. Keep in mind that the masterpiece is not finished with the stones: the plants will supply color and life.

Some gardeners don't plant until all the rocks are in place, but most can't help themselves and will plant while they set stone. This makes it easy to get a plant's roots into extremely narrow and deep crevices since they can be tucked in sideways – but never rely on plants for structural support. They don't live forever and cannot mortar your garden safely together.

Don't forget to add the odd flat rock for your coffee cup.

Every rock should look 'as if it belonged to the next, and had been its bed-fellow since the foundations of the hills were laid.'

Reginald Farrer, *The English Rock Garden*, 1919

Right: The rock placement in the garden of Vojtěch Holubec is so natural, that the plants appear to be growing on pure bedrock.

Step 7: Fill and top-dress crevices

Filling and top-dressing can be finicky and take just as much time as stonework. After you shovel in just enough soil to keep the stones from wiggling from side to side, fill up the crevices, trying to ensure there are no air pockets under the stones. If using sand, it will not compact to the detriment of the plants, so you can pound it, causing it to sink several inches, and then top it up again. You can also water the medium with a garden hose, but be mindful not to accidentally undermine your rockwork's support. The sunken grade of these freshly pounded crevices also gives opportunity to add different layers of custom soil mix, if desired. Fill the crevices almost to the rims of the stones, leaving about 2.5cm (1in) for top-dressing.

Poke all your rocks with your boots or walk over them to make sure none move, especially on steep slopes. If they do, the elements will slowly loosen and destabilize your garden, and it's much easier to fix them at this stage than when a fugitive rock is against a prized plant. Ideally, you would leave the garden to settle for at least the first winter. Plenty of builders do this, but most of us are impatient, so we must hand-settle the fill.

Stabilizing steep crevices

On steep vertical crevices, try setting your stones close together so that crevices are thin (those that are less steep can be wider). Gravel wider than the crevice can be mixed into the soil behind the stones so that it clogs the crevice like a sideways hourglass. Another traditional way to avoid erosion is to pound small slivers of rock into the spaces between the larger stones with a hammer or mallet so that their faces match that of the larger stones on either side. This is sometimes best done in conjunction with the actual planting of these crevices so that space is sufficient for each plant.

Starting at the bottom of a vertical crevice, pound in rock. The longer and thinner the better (like a spike), filling just a few inches of the crevice length but wide enough to fill the gap. Above that, plant a rooted cutting, seedling, or small potted plant, then

Closing a steep vertical crevice to avoid the soil sloughing out.

above that put in another sliver of rock. In a very long, steep crevice, this can be done a few times, leaving rock pieces between plants. Work your way up the steep crevice until you reach the top, at which point the vertical crevice is closed to erosion. One trick, especially if the slivers are too thin and don't fit perfectly, is to make a clay puck that fits the crevice and insert it before pounding in the rock. Then pound the rock into the clay puck. This helps to cement the rock in place and closes any gaps between the sliver and the adjoining rock, further precluding erosion.

The top-dressing

When top-dressing and planting the less steep sections of the garden, mix pieces of the same rock type as the full-sized stones with the gravel, or at least find top-dressing shards the same color as your main rock type. Since gravity is not as much of a problem on gentle slopes, they don't necessarily need to be pounded in unless their faces need to be made level with surrounding stones.

If you are fortunate enough to acquire crushed gravel of the same stone as your garden, you can just pour your fine gravel over the garden and brush it in with a broom. For the majority of your gravel, use a screened size under 1.25cm (½in), as it's easy to dig in and work with. Then mix in or top it with smaller amounts of larger screened sizes up to those as large as your smallest stones, giving the impression that the gravel is actively shedding from your stone.

You can settle the big, loose gravel on top of the fine gravel merely by stepping on it otherwise nature and time will settle it nicely, especially in winter conditions. Aim to make top-dressings about 2.5cm (1in) deep over any soil mix, but thicker and thinner areas are acceptable.

Observe and enjoy the change in sunlight and shadows over your crevice garden. See how lower basins dry slowly and high peaks dry quickly, and where weeds appear. Make a point to observe it in different seasons, too. If you have a cat or dog, it will often find the warm spots in winter and the cool spots in summer. It's only through accrued observation and trial and error that you will refine an understanding of your microclimates.

Top to bottom: Vertical crevices before closing with clay, plants, and rock slivers. Plants in place. Finishing the garden is one of the most satisfying aspects of construction. Top-dressing is the final stage of the construction process; use a variety of sizes for natural effect.

Step 8: Plant it!

A garden's first plants are the pioneers that will tell you how to proceed with future plantings. Many popular garden-center plants, such as miniature thymes, sempervivums, and campanulas, are easy to grow and tolerant of a wide variety of conditions. Start with these and slowly shift to smaller and more difficult plants as you discover your microclimates and refine your taste.

The main predictor of success is a plant's condition before planting. Inspect your purchases by gently tipping them out of their pots, looking for healthy, active root tips.

Plants that usually bloom in summer or fall don't grow much in the cool seasons and are always best planted in spring or early summer, but in climates where summer conditions test plants more than winter, fall planting gives the longest time to establish. If you have cool-season alpines to plant, for example, wintertime is also fine as long as your ground is not frozen.

Healthy young plants become healthy mature plants, as exemplified by this specimen of *Dianthus* 'Eleanor Parker'.

Bare-root planting.

The first plants in a new crevice garden instantly bring it to life.

Bare-root planting ensures quick establishment in a new home.

Getting the planting right is critical when there is a big difference between the pampered soil in a nursery-grown pot and the harsher lean soil in the garden. Most gardeners will wash all inappropriate soil off the plant so that the new roots will blend seamlessly when it is planted out. Some who grow their own stock engineer their home nursery mix to be easily knocked or rinsed off the roots.

Take note of where the crown of the potted plant is – the 'neck' where the stem and roots meet. Knock the plant out of its pot, and gently work off all or most of its potting mix; if the mix clings to the roots, rinse it off in a bucket of water. Then dig a hole the depth of the plant's dangling roots; deep is better than wide. Carefully lower the bare plant into the hole and hold it suspended so the crown is level with the soil level of the garden, *not* the top-dressing. Ensure the roots hang as deep as they can safely stretch and are also spread out a bit against a side (rather than dangling like a wet ponytail). You can guide them with your trowel or butter knife. Backfill part of your dirt into the hole, chasing it down with some clean water while still maintaining the plant's proper crown level. This brings the lowest roots into perfect intimate contact with your crevice garden mix and eliminates air pockets. Then backfill the rest of the hole with the remaining medium and water in the plant again. Bring gravel, rock chips or top-dressing back around the plant to hug its crown and tuck it in for a successful rooting-in.

Err on the side of planting deeply in gravel, because a plant can stretch but generally cannot shrink.

New plants should be diligently watered in to settle the soil, and watered regularly afterwards so their roots are never allowed to dry out until they can penetrate more deeply. If planting in hot, sunny summer conditions, above about 21°C (70°F), shade new plants temporarily for about two weeks to prevent them from shock, as the fine root hairs lost in planting must be replaced before they can hydrate themselves properly. Some people use pieces of burlap, chunks of wood, or even tiny tents of woven nursery shade cloth. Don't use black or dark material, as it will burn plants where it touches them.

Alternative and specialized planting

To plant species with wide or otherwise big heads – especially into a corner formed between two stones – try sliding over an entire slice of soil from the side of the hole to completely bury the roots from the side. This establishes the plant in one move and leaves an accessible hole next to it that is easier to back-fill. It just needs a good watering afterwards.

Occasionally, you may have a plant growing in a medium very similar to that which it is going into, in which case bare-rooting is not essential. If your medium is sandy or free-flowing, collapsing your planting hole as you dig, simply pre-wet the area before planting to stabilize and 'glue' it together.

For plants that seem to require a paper-thin crevice, try 'sandwich' planting – a technique we learned from plant-hunter and crevice-garden innovator Vojtěch Holubec. Lift two slabs out of the garden. Smear or paint their facing sides with clay or wet, sifted soil, as though you were putting clay mayonnaise in a rock sandwich. Spread out the bare-root system of your plant on this clay surface with the plant's head just hanging off the edge of the stone, then squish the two slabs together, leaving the plant's head sticking out from its incredibly tight home, and replace this 'sandwich' in the garden.

Rooted cuttings and young seedlings can also be planted directly into tight crevices or in small clay plugs in steep precarious crevices. Succulent cuttings can often be jammed into spots without roots. Some gardeners even root more difficult plants directly in the garden simply by timing planting with new root growth. The plants need to be babied a bit in the beginning, but will often become your longest-lived and best-performing plants since they are essentially starting their life in the garden, and have a root system built there. Tufa gardeners will often use a power drill with a masonry bit to create a small starting hole filled with clay or silt and capped with tufa dust around the plant.

Direct sowing of seeds is often unsuccessful because of the crevice garden's dry surface, but can produce the finest specimens if it works. Many plants will still grow and prosper where they cannot germinate on their own.

Planting seedlings soon after germination is one of the best ways to get plants established quickly.

How to plant a seedling

Planting a sensitive young acantholimon seedling to promote quick establishment.

1 Identify planting pocket.

2 Dig suitable hole.

3 Fill hole with water and allow to drain.

4 Gently plant seedling with roots dangling as deep as possible but keeping the crown of the plant at the crevice top.

5 Press around seedling gently but firmly to ensure it won't sink.

6 Top-dress to protect crown and foliage.

7 Water in to settle soil evenly around plant roots.

THE CREVICE GARDEN

LIVING WITH A CREVICE GARDEN

Crevice gardens tend to require more up-front effort to create but, once established, need far less maintenance than beds and borders, as the plants are slow-growing and long-lived. In general, maintenance tends to decrease over time as plants mature, soil settles, and problem plants are ousted.

Kirsten Andersen's garden near Aarhus, Denmark provides easy maintenance years after the hard work of construction is complete.

Labelling plants

The value of many rock garden plants derives from their provenance, so consider options for cataloguing and labeling plants that have been devised by clever rock gardeners:

· Bury plastic tags under gravel to avoid sun bleaching, or hide them under the nearest loose stone.
· Place tags in some orientation related to the plant, for example, 'always buried to the north'.
· Use enamel to paint a plant's index number on the head of a nail driven in next to it.
· Emboss copper strips and staple them to the ground in front of the plant.
· Sink screws, which resist heaving out of the soil, whose color blends with the rocks.
· Use graphite pencil (B6) on plant labels.
· Keep a digital record that can include the genus, species, site in the garden, source or locality, common name, color, expected height, date planted, number planted, size of pot, location in the garden, general notes, and date dead.

Tools for the crevice garden

Don't scoff until you've tried them!
· Hori-hori or Japanese gardening knives
· Rockery trowel or widgers
· Rust-proof, thrift-store butterknives
· Flat-head screwdrivers
· Forceps
· Tweezers
· Chopsticks
· Metal salad tongs (for spined plants)
· Veterinary surgical tongs (for spiny or toxic plants)
· Hand rake (plastic is less damaging to plants) or small broom
· Trenching shovel and sharp-shooter (for jobs requiring the full power of a shovel)
· Leaf blower
· Utility vacuum (pro tip: finesse will be required)
· Your hands (best rake, ever)

Right: A selection of useful crevice garden tools: dandelion weeder, narrow trowel, hori-hori knife, yankee weeder, shallow trowel, rock hammer, butterknife, screwdriver, dibber, secateurs.

Irrigation

The mimicry of rain is essential, since the movement of water is a major element of the crevice. The frequency and amount of water will be determined by your plants, climate, and soil. Generally, it's needed when the local precipitation is short of what plants would expect in their homelands. Plants in containers will always need more than those in the ground unless they are deliberately dryer. Poke your finger or a wooden skewer deep into a crevice to check true moisture. Hand-watering is best for new plants and small gardens. It is the most 'water-wise' and easiest to adjust for spot-watering, season, and weather. Tufa retains internal moisture, often without overhead water, but will generally need more constant water than adjacent gardens. These stones have to be monitored by touching them – they are perceptibly cooler when generously hydrated.

Below: A dandelion weed in a sidewalk (pavement) crack.

Prevent the spread of bacteria, fungi, and even crawling parasites by sterilizing your equipment with lighters, rubbing alcohol (isopropyl), and even aerosol air freshener/disinfectant. Bulbs are particularly susceptible to viruses transferred by dirty blades.

Some watering will be key to establishing young plants.

139

Weeds

Rocky surfaces preclude most weed germination and establishment, but constant vigilance is required to keep the few persistent ones out. You'll notice seed-borne weeds will be limited to those with taproots. Be extra diligent in pulling or rooting out perennial running grasses, field bindweed, horsetail, and other rhizomatous spreaders. At a minimum, weeds should never be allowed to drop seed. Impossible plants can be treated by painting or sponging with a herbicide before the dormant season, though we recommend chemical treatment only after exhausting all other means of eradication.

Top: Many saxatile plants such as *Saxifraga burseriana* require no fertilizer to grow well.
Bottom: Other plants, for example *Gentiana acaulis*, are greedy and will benefit from fertilization.

Fertilizing

Over-fertilizing saxatile plants often sends them 'out of character', causing leggy growth, suppressed bloom, disease, or rot. Exceptions are when replacing lost water-soluble nutrients in wet climates or to accelerate the growth of nursery plants. It is essential to fertilize potted plants because they can't reach more nutrition. When commencing a fertilizing regime, always start with a little and slowly increase until you see a good response. Rock garden plants generally take half-strength or weaker dilutions of most fertilizers. Organic fertilizers may promote pathogens by creating a humate-rich soil, though this is less the case with chemical or mineral fertilizers.

Cleaning and pruning

Cleanliness is critical in the crevice garden. If fallen leaves and debris are left to decompose and incorporate into the soil, they void the function of rocky microclimates. In wet winter climates, cut herbaceous vegetation back sooner to avoid wintertime rot. In dry or severe winter areas, prune before plants start putting on new spring growth. Herbs may also be cut back after they go to seed. Deadhead cushions and buns by gently patting or rubbing them to knock off the tiny flower stems – use leather gloves when patting your acantholimons. Some gardeners use an outdoor vacuum or broom to easily groom cushion plants. Keep in mind that standing and attached dead material provides winter bird food, nesting material, decorative seeds/stems, and protection for the plant through winter.

If a bun threatens to consume a valuable neighbor plant, lift the edges gently and prune it. If it is a firm bun with an inflexible grip on the rocks or earth below, use a knife or the blade-side of the pruner, diving in from above and at an angle. Dust worrisome wounds with sulfur or otherwise air dry to heal. If an old acantholimon bites the dust, and you don't want the hassle of disposing of its thorny carcass, set it on fire where it sits.

Pluck out dead sections of buns and other long-lived plants. Some gardeners fill the void with gravel or stones to keep the tight form of the plant, and very often the scar is covered over by the growth of adjacent rosettes. Conifers and other woody shrubs can be kept small by candling them – snapping their new growth tips partially or fully in spring before the new needles have grown out. Older specimens can be maintained as pseudo-bonsai by aggressive thinning, exposing the maturing trunk and inside branch structure. Maturing woody shrubs that shade out other desirables can be trained (sooner rather than later) to lean away from the middle of the crevice garden.

Pests and diseases

Ants are the most universal pest, and while they generally don't attack plants, they wreak havoc on the plants' real estate. Spring ant excavations undermine stones and plants, sometimes removing or burying plants or even removing all the soil from roots. Soil worked intensively by ants often repels water, depriving the garden of moisture. Deter ants with a little more irrigation, bait or trap them (to avoid poisoning other insects), or flood their entries with soapy water. Or, you might just allow ants to attract birds, for which they are food.

Voles and mice may also menace crevice gardens by eating plants and seeds and creating intricate burrows protected by the stones. With any luck, the warm rocks will attract garden snakes, too, keeping them in check. Problematic slugs can also be baited or hunted at night with a headlamp.

Regardless of cause, always perform a 'plant autopsy' to determine what was damaged first – leaves, crown, or roots. The crevice garden's warm, dry environment discourages fungus and bacteria, but aphids, true bugs, grasshoppers, vegetarian beetles and others may attack both healthy and sick plants. Be sure to try natural remedies before reaching for systemic pesticides.

Propagation: grow your own

Exotic plants are not commonly available at retail outlets, and this is even more true of crevice garden plants. As rock gardeners become more experienced, they naturally seek choicer and rarer species, expanding their hunt for seeds in catalogs, seed exchanges, personal correspondence, and in natural areas where it is legal to collect them. Some regions are lucky enough to have rock garden plant nurseries, and we're lucky to be alive at a time when the internet allows us to mail-order plants and seeds.

Nevertheless, beyond growing the widest variety of plants, there are other advantages to home propagation. You can grow specimens to a small size that fit more easily in a crevice and establish more readily. You can also harvest and germinate seeds of plants that have already proved themselves in your garden to have mass plantings of them. You might also inadvertently preserve and improve 'bloodlines' that may be quite at home in your area but rare elsewhere. What's even more fun is that you can breed or select for new colors, tougher strains, and smaller or prettier forms. Finally, seed saving and propagation ensure you'll have extra plants for your own garden's succession, as well as some for sharing with friends and trading at plant sales.

The three main methods of propagation – division, cuttings, and seed – require just a few basic tools, such as a cold frame, a small alpine house, or even a bucket of sand covered with a piece of glass.

Division

Any plant that grows roots from new stems as it expands is a perfect candidate for division, which is exactly what the word implies; you just dig up part of the plant and rip it into pieces with each piece having its own roots. Division also produces a clone of the mother, so you know you're getting exactly the same plant.

There are two techniques for division. For carpeting plants that root as they travel, such as *Arenaria* ex. 'Wallowa Mountain', dig material from the edge of the plant. The outer growth is the youngest and most vigorous part and most likely to establish successfully. Digging up the outer portion also leaves the mother plant relatively undisturbed and, if performed carefully, will not be noticeable. Many plants such as nailwort, sempervivums, and even some choice silver saxifrages are easily and quickly propagated this way.

The second type of division involves digging up the whole plant. Those that form dense crowns over time, such as *Primula* or *Ramonda,* respond best to this type of propagation. A little more care must be taken because each individual crown will have its own set of roots, which must not be damaged. The basic technique is to dig up the plant and wash off all the soil so that you can clearly see the individual crowns. Once clean, these crowns, with their associated roots, can be gently teased apart, or separated with a sharp knife.

141

With the right technique, a single, special saxifrage can be propagated in good numbers.

Haberlea rhodopensis is easily divided.

Although either type of division will work at any time of the year, the best time for both is late winter to early spring, just as the plant is breaking dormancy. In this way, the plant barely notices what's happened and the gardener can enjoy its blooms that year. All newly divided plants should be given full attention during their first year.

It is also a great time to divide plants when renovating, rebuilding, or expanding the rock garden, as often older, dividable plants are being dug anyway. Doing this produces many plants that can then be replanted as colonies for a natural look, lending real integrity to the garden.

Some plants cannot be propagated in this way due to their basic physiology, such as those attached to a main woody stem. Trying to divide these would be the equivalent of dividing a tree, spelling certain death. Some research will always be necessary before choosing which propagation method is best for any given species.

Taking cuttings

This is simply a matter of taking a part of the plant (usually a single rosette or stem tip) and encouraging it to grow roots. Like division, cuttings guarantee that you get the same genetic material as that of the mother plant. While not as fast-maturing as divisions, cuttings produce good numbers of plants in a short time.

Taking cuttings is simple, but timing is very important. They fall into three basic categories: (1) softwood cuttings, taken of the newest, softest growth early in the spring; (2) semi-hardwood cuttings of semi-ripe wood taken midsummer; and (3) hardwood cuttings that are taken any time after the current year's stems have fully ripened. All three methods involve slightly different care and will take varying times to root, depending on the timing, species, and method used.

Easily Divided Plants

- *Delosperma congestum*
- *Erigeron scopulinus*
- *Gentiana acaulis*
- *Globularia cordifolia*
- *Haberlea rhodopensis*
- *Iris pumila*
- *Polygala chamaebuxus*
- *Ramonda myconi*
- *Raoulia australis*
- *Saxifraga cochlearis*
- *Sempervivum arachnoideum*
- *Teucrium pyrenaicum*

Typically, softwood cuttings taken early in the growing season root extremely quickly (10–30 days) but are often the most difficult because the young tissue involved is more susceptible to desiccation and disease. Some form of bottom heat and high humidity is necessary. Semi-hard cuttings are taken after the new growth is hard enough to snap, rather than crimp, when bent. Depending on the species, these grow roots very quickly due to warmer summer temperatures, and tend not to require bottom heat as much. Six to eight weeks is often the wait time for many semi-hard cuttings taken in summer, which is perfect timing for potting up for a fall plant sale, or direct fall planting into the crevice garden.

Hardwood cuttings root more slowly and are often left in the cold frames and potted on in the spring or following summer. Some form of rooting hormone may increase the success rate with certain plants. If you are unsure about timing and you have access to enough material, take cuttings every two weeks throughout the season and see what works best for the species you're growing.

The easiest way to keep humidity high is to cover the cold frame with a sheet of glass so that it's relatively airtight – effectively a greenhouse. An angled sheet of glass ensures that the cuttings don't get 'rained' on, as condensed water won't fall directly from above.

After timing, the second most important factor for success is to keep the frames out of direct sunlight – what you want is the brightest shade possible. Open the frames each day to let in some fresh air. The medium inside them can vary depending on what you're trying to grow, but for a wide range of rock garden plants, coarse sand is perfectly acceptable. Other possible rooting media are pumice, peat, perlite, or mixes and alternatives. The humid environment may be too moist for some dry-land plants that may rot before taking root, in which case just prop open your enclosure a bit for these. Bottom heat is optional for certain plants and speeds up the process.

Fall cuttings are easy to maintain and often root by spring, while most spring and summer cuttings will grow roots within eight weeks. Top-growth is often (but not always) an indication that the cutting has rooted. To check, give a gentle tug on the cuttings; the rooted ones will resist. Once carefully dug out, they may then be potted on or planted directly into the crevice garden and protected.

143

Above: A rooted cutting of *Daphne petraea*.
Right: A home-made cutting frame, made from a plastic tub covered by a piece of glass, is kept out of direct sunlight.

Seed

Growing from seed is the most common way rock gardeners enrich their gardens. Plants grown from seed will have some degree of variation and could potentially be a hybrid, especially if the seed is garden-collected. Nevertheless, this is the very best and sometimes only way to acquire plants when vegetative propagation is not possible. Many crevice gardeners participate in seed exchanges offered by various rock garden clubs, or buy from established seed companies. Wild-collected seed usually guarantees that the plant will come true to type, but be sure to collect seed at the right time, once it has fully ripened.

It is crucial that seed is stored properly if not sowed right away. Dry storage in an airtight container in the cool environment of the fridge or basement is the best chance for longevity and prevents the seeds from breaking dormancy. However, fresh seed is best, and a few species should be sown as soon as their seeds are ripe. A few absolutely must not dry out and should be sown immediately. Many temperate bulbs are particularly sensitive, as they are meant to germinate in the fall. Most seed, however, can be cleaned, shared, stored, and sown until midwinter to experience cold or freeze–thaw cycles and snow cover that trigger them to germinate in the spring.

The majority of alpine seeds need some amount of cold stratification (storing somewhere cold and moist) and, if they are not sown outdoors 3–8 weeks before spring, it's best to wait until the next fall. If you live in a cold continental climate, direct sowing outdoors is perfect to satisfy the number of chilling hours needed for germination. For winters in balmy climates, cold stratification is needed to mimic the winter conditions experienced by the seed in its natural home. Do this by storing moist seeds in the refrigerator, usually for one to three months. To save space for food and beer, put each species in a zip-lock bag with a moist piece of paper towel or a small amount of moist vermiculite. Seeds must be watched closely as, once their chilling requirements have been met, many will germinate in the fridge, making them difficult to deal with later.

Some seeds have a hard, thick coat which needs to be damaged to allow germination, a process known as scarification. *Astragalus* and *Convolvulus* will often require this treatment. Some folks use sandpaper or nick them with a file. 'Double dormant' species require both stratification and scarification. Just a few taxa are serotinous germinators, triggered by forest fire in nature, requiring alchemistic rituals of smoke and time in the oven to be conjured into seedlings at home.

144

Globularia incanescens is one of many plants that are easy to grow from seed.

Starting plants from seed is not only rewarding and quicker than you might think, it's also the only way to acquire certain plants.

Larger seeds that require soaking overnight or for several days may call for scarification. Soaking allows the seed coat to soften, and also leaches out any germination-inhibiting hormones that might be present. Use small vials or teacups for this simple operation. Adding a tiny drop of dish soap can help water penetrate the seed coat. Some seeds will float, but many will sink. Floating seeds may just need more time before they sink to the bottom and swell visibly larger, but floating is also a potential indication of non-viability; even though they may all look alike, some seeds may in fact be just an empty husk. If soaking for multiple days, change the water every twenty-four hours to lose those germination inhibitors.

For germinating difficult or old seed, some growers swear by gibberellic acid (also known as GA-3), a potent hormone that will reliably break dormancy. But be careful: overdosage will cause seedling etiolation or even death.

Consult germination guides to see which species demand which treatments, but most gardeners start sowing seed outdoors in winter, usually before February, to ensure that average cold stratification needs are met.

Sowing seed

Choose a loose seedling mix. Most rock gardeners start with a basic, commercial seed-starting mix and cut it with 50 percent sand or perlite for aeration. Fill small pots to just below the rim to allow for settling. Gently pack the soil down so that it won't settle when watered. A fine layer of sifted mix can help to smooth a coarse, chunky mix. Then sow the seeds on top of the medium. Sowing thinly will make it easier to prick out seedlings; large seeds may be spaced individually. Cover or bury large seeds to a depth about 3 times their size, but fine seeds need only the cover of a fine top-dressing of grit, approximately 3–5 mm (1/8in) screen size. Finally, gently water them in. Very small, dust-like seeds, such as some saxifrage species, need as much light as possible to germinate. To help keep these tiny seeds on the surface, apply the grit first, before sprinkling the seeds like dust over it. To avoid washing them away, soak the pots from the bottom by placing them in a tray of water.

The next step

Once the seeds are sown and watered, leave the pots outside to expose the seeds to good air circulation and the temperature fluctuations that occur in nature. A brightly lit but protected spot works well. If your location could be affected by violent rain or hail, leaf litter, or digging rodents, protect your pots in a cold frame, wire mesh frame, or unheated greenhouse or garage. Out of the snow or rain, they must be checked regularly to be kept damp throughout the winter and summer. Outdoors, a nice snowdrift built up on top of your seed pots is beneficial, supplying insulation and then moisture. For some northern hemisphere gardeners this is an east or north shadow of their house, This area may also be your best spot in summer to grow your seedlings until they are large enough to be planted. Alternatively, indoor propagation under lights is a great way to fill boring winter days or basement space, when you can give young plants closer attention and control the environment more strictly.

Potting mixes for growing new plants

The considerations for choosing or making a soil or soilless mix for small containers is similar to choosing one for a trough or garden except that its service time is truly temporary – just long enough to support a plant until it is planted in its permanent home – so there's less pressure on it. Short-lived perlite may be used instead of long-lived scoria, for instance. Media for growing up tiny plants are usually fairly nutrient-inert, relying on fertilizer to supply nutrients when needed, but not before, because tiny seedlings and cuttings are much more at risk of rotting in a nutritious or compost-enriched mix. They are generally grown lean until they have developed enough roots to demand feeding and resist infection.

You can take the guesswork out of this process by test-mixing small amounts of your potting mix. Put it in a pot and water it; observe its absorption and drainage. You can even up-end the pot and see if it has absorbed the water yet preserved some tiny air spaces for plant roots to breathe.

Cleanliness – of equipment, space, and potting medium – is next to godliness when it comes to propagation. The still, moist air inside a cold frame can create perfect conditions for detrimental fungi, and the lush growth of fresh seedlings could become an all-you-can-eat salad bar for slugs in a single night. Sterilize reused pots, pruners, and knives. Keep fungus at bay with decent air circulation. Open cold frames occasionally to let the fresh air in and use a fan in an alpine house. Air circulation not only helps to ward off fungal pathogens, but seedlings are strengthened by being blown around a bit.

A lot of propagation, especially for the beginner, is experimental. If a cutting doesn't root for you at one time of the year, try it at a different time, and record your dates and strategies. Lastly, be sure to hold onto your seed pots for more than one year (ideally two or three). Some species may wait years to germinate.

There are many more advanced techniques such as tissue culture, leaf cuttings, grafting, and twin-scaling, but most plants can be easily multiplied using one of these three basic methods. So fill your world with lots of great plants!

In the end, a garden's purpose is for you – to please, to challenge, to reward, and to humble. Crevice gardens offer a long-form conversation with every aspect of backyard nature, from weather to physics, chemistry, geology, botany, and wildlife. Together, they whisper of the gentle peace and permanence of rocky places.

Telesonix jamesii in a small crevice container.

The Cornell Mix

· *1 part peat (limed) or alternative (e.g. coir, conifer compost)*
· *1 part perlite*
· *1 expectation to fertilize*

This simple formula grows a staggering array of plants in production greenhouses and can be safely watered with a heavy hand to little detriment.

The NARGS

· *1 part peat or alternative (e.g. coir, conifer compost)*
· *1 part perlite*
· *1 part sand*

Plants can be transplanted in and out of this well because of the loose sand. It's a proven recipe, but it is possible to overwater seedling desert dwellers.

Kenton's Trinity

· *1 part readymade peat-based mix or alternative (e.g. coir, conifer compost)*
· *1 part scoria (or perlite in a pinch)*
· *1 part expanded shale or similar*

A versatile mix which is clean for tender seedlings but has water- and air-holding capacity to buffer babies against erratic watering/weather. It works well for cacti in containers as well as alpines, which are picky about good drainage but susceptible to drying out.

Cornell Light

· *2 parts perlite*
· *1 part peat or readymade soilless mix*

This simple formula grows a staggering array of plants in production greenhouses and can be safely watered with a heavy hand to little detriment.

CASE STUDIES: LESSONS FROM THE BEST

Their universal nature and the variety of problems they solve will mean that crevice gardens and their creators will express themselves in a myriad of ways. Each will deal with their own constraints and fulfill their own unique goal. From home pocket gardens to large public spaces, we offer a suite of stories of real gardens and real people in real places to bring home the overwhelming range of possibilities. We particularly try to highlight innovations that will (or have already) spark(ed) their own genre of crevice, and invite you to build upon and explore beyond what has gone before. We hope this range of successful examples will embolden gardeners working in similar places.

Zdeněk Zvolánek's Beauty Slope enjoys enough space to repeat plants and provide sufficient variety for season-long color.

A jewel box for a small space

Linda moved to Denver to be closer to family, leaving a third of an acre in Portland, Oregon, that she had gardened for 20 years. Her new townhouse has a very narrow side garden, no more than 5m (16ft) across, facing south against a two-story home, an aspect that creates a veritable solar oven in summer. In Portland she grew large perennials, but just a few of such plants would have filled her new space, which would have been boring – so she joined the local rock garden club, where she learned about small plants for the Colorado climate.

She quickly filled her little garden with two small shade trees to counter the merciless heat, a couple of vegetable beds, some perennials, a fountain, and a rock garden mound. The rock garden was dominated by native penstemons and was completely full, with 20–30 plants. There was no more room in the garden, so Linda resorted to planting in the alley until she learned about crevice gardens when she hosted a rock garden lecturer on the topic. Lured by the promise of growing more 'weird and interesting' plants, especially in a small space, Linda hired some help to set a number of stones and make a small crevice garden in a corner. Enjoying that, she decided to replace her entire main rock garden mound with a crevice garden, too.

Unafraid of risk, Linda decided to experiment and made the first crevice garden in the area to have a mix of half gravel and half sand (which had hitherto been assumed too dry or infertile) on top of her existing rich clay topsoil. Her crevice garden is four tons of sandstone rocks laid directly against one another to

gain a maximum height of 1.2m (4ft). One side returns gently to the ground, where rock plants blend with ground covers and perennials. The majority of the crevice garden is a gentle north slope, so the tops of plants are in plenty of sun, but their bases and earth are in shadow because of the shape of the garden. The plants are shown off with gentle backlighting for much of the year.

Linda planted the little garden with dozens of varied plants over several years, as it could absorb a lot. Many died, from which she learned where the microclimates are, and she now manages to have cacti and gentians growing within 1m (3ft) of one another. She grows classic cushion plants beautifully and to a compact size, with good blooming. Using a flat screwdriver as her tool, she plants in the narrowest cracks she can, and estimates that her garden holds about 75–100 plants. In her search for broad diversity, she built herself a bog, and a tufa garden for saxifrages. She waters the garden once every 7–10 days in summer, and puts on a simple, micro-spray watering timer when she goes on holidays.

What keeps her interested? The learning experience and challenge, she says, and the enjoyment of trying to make everything she bought grow. She has observed that not all newer plants in the garden thrive as well as the old ones, perhaps because some introductions are satisfied with the mineral soil and others need more nutrients, so she will test fertilizing certain plants. She advises new crevice gardeners, 'It's trial and error. Don't give up.'

Drabas, opposite, are the first to bloom, but whatever the season, tall rockwork casts alluring long shadows, above.

Next page: Boundless variety in a tiny space grabs visitors' attention.

Far Reaches Farm

Alpines in wet winters

The charming town of Port Townsend, at the northeast foot of the Olympic Mountains in Washington state, is the home of this rare plant mail-order nursery and the associated Far Reaches Botanical Conservancy. Owners Kelly Dodson and Sue Milliken are specialists who make frequent plant exploration trips to Asia and beyond, often just ahead of voracious urban expansion. They grow and sell their plants from the FRBC collection, which in turn helps to subsidize their non-profit plant conservancy in an effort to preserve rare plants that have a bleak future in nature. Their charitable mission has attracted volunteers in critical roles at the nursery and conservancy, such as financial manager and taxonomist.

In the spring of 2019, Sue and Kelly invited us to build a crevice garden on the nursery's grounds that would serve as a mother-plant garden, educational program, and fundraiser for the conservancy. Rock gardening was not new to them – in fact Sue had been an alpine plant specialist before they formed the nursery. To maximize the number of crevices, they forewent cheaper local rock in favor of hand-picked palletized sandstone brought all the way from eastern Montana, which has an irregular slab-like shape that could create extreme topography.

The first problem for alpine and rock plants in the Pacific Northwest is wet winters. The second is surprisingly dry summers – even more so for rain-shadowed Port Townsend, where the annual 45cm (18in) of mainly winter rain is half that of nearby Seattle. This is where the excellent drainage yet deep stored water of a classic crevice garden serves well. The crevices at Far Reaches are filled with pure sand 10–25cm (4–10in) deep, below which is a well-amended and free-draining, originally heavy, local soil. In a fortuitous miscommunication, we started to build another garden mound on top of a stored pile of crushed basalt gravel screened 5mm (¼in) and less that had been intended for driveway use, accidentally locking in this experimental medium. It worked so well Kelly and Sue will probably use it for future crevice beds.

The couple employ the crevice garden to grow many things, but most importantly, Olympic Mountain endemics – from seed ethically collected outside the national park – the future existence of which is severely threatened by climate change in their very niche habitats. These include *Veronica dissecta* ssp. *lanuginosa* (formerly *Synthyris pinnatifida* ssp. *lanuginosa*), which thrives in both substrates. The elusive northwest American *Paeonia brownii* joins the ranks, while overhangs in the garden were designed toward a growing collection of cacti and mesembs (Aizoaceae), unlikely plants to see outdoors in the Pacific Northwest. Only time will tell what new plants Kelly and Sue can house, share, and conserve with their crevice garden.

This crevice garden, opposite, is large enough to have scale against shrubs, lawn, and home, and its height also lifts small plants, above, to eye level.

RHS Wisley

An educational tool for the public

The crevice garden at the Royal Horticultural Society Garden Wisley in Surrey, UK, may be one of the most influential of its type, being among the earliest public crevice gardens in the English-speaking world and enjoying visitors from all parts of the globe. It was built in 2010 by staff and Zdeněk Zvolánek during the alpine curatorship of Paul Cumbleton, who is renowned as an expert on growing plants from *Pleione* to *Massonia*, so his talent and skill in cultivating diversity was the perfect fit for the strengths of a crevice garden. Just two years after its creation, this garden contained 700 plants.

It is made of 42 tonnes (46 US tons) of sandstone from a quarry in the Forest of Dean, covering about 78sq m (840sq ft), with the crevices filled with pure sand. Narrow paths cut into its tall and dramatic form, creating nearly wall-like edges that necessitated using metal bar and some poured concrete to keep them stable. Initial planting took a wide, liberal, and experimental approach, since no one knew exactly what would work. Ten years on, there are two essential categories of plants: basic, colorful crowd-pleaser plants such as *Aubretia*, *Aurinia*, and *Alyssum*, then hidden, esoteric gems, for example *Morisia monanthos* and *Androsace lanuginosa*. Very small plants are raised up closer to eye level like tiny jewels on display and planted near paths, rather than further into the bed where they are harder to see. Instead, those areas are dominated by larger alpines such as daphnes, *Erigeron glaucus*, and *Phlox subulata*.

Chloe Bidwell (pictured right) has been on the Alpine Team since arriving at Wisley a month before

the crevice garden was built. She has learned that the garden certainly provides a special environment that plant groups such as saxatile *Campanula* and *Dianthus* thrive in – especially in vertical cracks – that a traditional garden bed cannot, and it creates an extreme array of microclimates – in fact the highest crevices are so dry it is hard to get plants established in them. Chloe also notes that plants grow more in the natural character that they would in nature. But the crevice garden doesn't accommodate everything the gardeners try to grow; penstemons generally dislike the place and the garden cannot completely escape the warm, wet winters of Surrey.

Reflecting on the garden, Chloe regards her main role as being an educator to students and the public as to what alpine plants are. The crevice garden provides a context where plants can be seen growing among rocks on a mountain-like feature, allowing her to teach the ecology of alpine plants and their adaptations to life above tree line. She says that where it excels is in the stunning sculptural effect that draws visitors in. Chloe and her staff also enjoy this immersion in the garden – while weeding, being in

the garden plays with your perspective, drawing you into the microcosm, almost like being underwater. 'It's incredibly therapeutic,' she says.

Left: Chloe fills crevices during construction.
Above: Multiples of *Thymus* 'Bressingham' provide eye-catching color at a distance.
Below: The raised form, embraced by paths, lifts small plants right up to the noses of visitors and students.

ZZ's Beauty Slope

A masterpiece borne of restraint

Zdeněk Zvolánek may be the father of modern crevice gardening, having championed the style more widely than anyone else to date. It is only fitting to take lessons from his home garden, which is not the intimidating, unreproducible masterwork of a skilled superhuman, but an educational example of a man cleverly making the most of a difficult site. He urges us to see it this way and take a lesson from it.

'ZZ', as his friends know him, is a retired railroad man. His family home is in Karlík, a village just outside Prague. The humble, three-story dwelling is embedded in a steep slope against forest service land. It faces south in a relatively dry summer area for Europe. The slope exists because of an underlayment of local karst rock, which has even been historically quarried nearby, and from which ZZ still draws material. The house takes up the whole width of the property, so the garden rises behind it. One must walk up a flight of stairs and through the patio to access it, which prevents him from carrying anything more than armloads of any material in or out. Everything must be sourced on site; he uses only rock found on or near the property, building mounds between the zigzagging pathways to bring the best gems closer to view. There is no crushed gravel brought in, but collections of chipped rock only where needed. He shamelessly uses sempervivums like glue, with their shallow roots, to knit loose soil in crevices.

The steepness is akin to an average staircase, so it is not surprising that the garden is serviced by a path that is almost pure steps until it reaches a landing of somewhat level earth higher up, above the roofline of

the house. A traditional gardener may have suffered from the stress of feeling they had to fight their garden's soil washing away, perhaps even the hillside sliding off, but ZZ knows that a crevice garden is an ideal rock-hard solution to his steep slope, which he calls the Beauty Slope.

Below and opposite: ZZ's Beauty Slope exists in an abandoned medieval quarry from which stone was used in the building of Prague.

There are a few small trees and shrubs that provide shade on the level area, accommodating those alpines that are not as xeric. The path zigzags up the hill only single-file wide, paved with irregular buried rock and looking every bit like a mountain hiking trail, with plants even growing right in the middle of the path. The zigzag of the path also creates tiny north-facing aspects when it cuts minimally into the slope, rebelling against the otherwise totally southern aspect. Here, cool-loving plants hide from the summer heat and are at the very feet of garden visitors.

Less accessible and dangerously steep areas are saturated with tough sub-shrubs such as *Aethionema grandiflorum* and *Moltkia petraea*, which are low-maintenance and repeatable, creating an expansive view of seasonal colors. ZZ refers to these moments as 'the pink time' or 'the blue time', when masses of colour unify the garden. In spring and fall, the only sensible times of year, he transplants seedlings to fill any open soil and further exclude weeds.

ZZ does not irrigate his established garden, only watering new plants with collected rainwater. In this way, his garden is dominated by plants that are satisfied with the local climate, so ZZ is free to travel without worrying about watering. More moisture-loving plants live in low, shady pockets or in balcony pots.

The whole area is dominated by short plants and a few tall ones, leaving an open, mountainous vibe while preserving views to and from the garden. Something is in bloom nearly every month of the year. Bulbs grow between and under the leafy plants, while new seedlings are nurtured in the shade of his balcony.

When an area is dominated by an old plant, or one species, it's an opportunity to tear it out and freshen up the area, expose buried stones and diversify plantings. Turkish, Balkan, Mediterranean, and American plants seem most at home in ZZ's garden, so he constantly tries new taxa from those places.

ZZ does not fight the strong limitations in his garden, those of site, heat, and drought, but instead leverages them to advantage, creating not an edifice of struggle and dominance over nature but a relaxed garden in harmony with nature, rich with precious plants.

Dwarf seedling of *Daphne schlyteri*.

Paul Cumbleton

Pockets for the choicest plants

Having been curator of alpine collections at RHS Wisley, Paul Cumbleton has a lot of experience from his care of the crevice garden there. After he ended his career as a public gardener he retired to Somerset, where he built a crevice garden to suit his own fancies. Paul was always a wizard at accommodating the very specific needs of plants, and now his personal focus can be on the plants themselves, rather than trying to recreate a mountain exhibit for the public. He took a few observations from Wisley to inform his own garden: the sand in the Wisley garden had the kind of texture that rendered it hydrophobic when totally dry, so water would frustratingly run off it. The sand also left many of the plants at Wisley needing regular fertilizing. However, Paul observed that 'sand reduces the disease pressure by reducing the places for disease to live,' so the main mound of his crevice garden is a mix of sand, grit, and dolomitic crushed fines for better mineral nutrition. He says he can tell when plants have grown through this and reached into the soil below by their sudden vigor. His rock is a local bright gray limestone, and he has left regular spaces between the strata, which he chose to give playful curves. It's top-dressed with a layer of broken chunks of the same limestone.

Paul enjoys trying new and unusual plants in his crevice garden. Employing his evenly spaced crevices, he will often create a pocket of a different soil for new plantings to give them a head start or address their specific needs. He grows European alpines, Mediterranean saxatile plants, and American desert plants side by side. Most impressive might be the variety of *Castilleja* species he has grown which have bloomed with and without host plants. Usually, this genus must be grown under the dry protection of glass in the UK. He has found that the most vigorous and persistent are species which come from the most similar climates, like the coastal Californian *Castilleja latifolia*.

Iris reichenbachii

Due to the mineral mix underlying the garden and its various pockets, certain plants are completely satisfied and others are not, so Paul fertilizes certain plants twice a year with all-purpose powdered feed. Especially hungry plants may get additional liquid fertilizer on the same regimes as container-grown plants. He identifies his plants by writing the names on the bottom of the nearest stone with a marker rather than using labels.

Unusually for crevice gardens, Paul does not focus on bun and cushion plants, but prefers petite herbaceous plants or evergreens with fascinating flower structure. A master of cultivating plants, he could grow anything, but he grows what gives him pleasure. In his home garden, on a heavy clay loam, he and his partner have room to grow large perennials and shrubs, and they have a glasshouse each for keeping bulb collections.

Isolated patches of custom-made soils are completely invisible under Paul's diverse and playful plant collection of personal favourites.

Synthetic forms in a human landscape

There are no mountains near Utrecht in the northern Netherlands from which to take inspiration, nor indeed even rocks for a rock garden. The Dutch have gained much of their land from the sea, and the area around Utrecht was marsh until it was dried out. So the rock garden at the Utrecht University Botanic Gardens started with stones shipped from Belgium in the 1960s but more recently, through budget-motivated innovation, a corner of it has been enriched with a cheaper product that is readily available: concrete. This innovation is historically huge, since legitimizing the use of concrete for rock gardening smashes the problem of stone availability: there are indeed places on Earth where getting stone is just not feasible. It levels the playing field so that rock gardening is possible anywhere humans live.

Exploring a new concept's possibilities in the full spirit of Dutch ingenuity, the crevice gardens at Utrecht may be the only ones that can claim to have every aspect in relation to the sun, as they have been built as spheres. Wiert Nieuman, the head gardener who designed them, did not attempt to make concrete impersonate a natural rock, but instead embraced a shape that looks like the whole Earth. The spheres have a novelty and character that grabs even the least botanically oriented visitors, with their weight seemingly suspended in a compelling tension with gravity.

A nearby crevice wall is set on the diagonal, with occasional stripes of precious natural stone, accentuating its height. It is a mixture of modern art, masonry, and garden that exemplifies the use of a crevice garden as a wall, putting something decorative and alive in a space that could have been cold and industrial. This inventive theme is repeated in the rock garden, where concrete sewer pipes are used as massive raised beds for alpine plants, their forms exposed and celebrated rather than camouflaged.

Below and opposite: The spherical forms at Utrecht University Botanic Gardens are made from recycled concrete.

Current Head Gardener Gerard van Buiten says that when the spheres were constructed in the mid-1990s, wooden forms were used to maintain their roundness. The axis was a metal irrigation pipe. Latitudinal bands of roof tile slate intruded into the otherwise solid sphere of common concrete paving slabs. But a unique problem arose: the soil would surely be smashed between the heavy layers and made inhospitable to plants. Worse yet, as its organic components broke down, this 'mortar' would no longer be in place between the concrete. So another ingenious idea arose: scoria – porous volcanic gravel – was mixed into the medium. A hard granitic gravel would have also supported the layers like tiny shorings, but scoria is permeable, offering even better paths for air, water, and plant roots to penetrate into the spheres.

Demure and fragrant *Daphne arbuscula* grows right at nose-level, and any plants growing below the 'equator' of these spheres hang eye-catchingly away from their seats. Here also the unique advantage of a sphere-shaped garden proves itself with more than a decade's success with fickle *Dionysia aretioides*, which has a reputation for disliking rain on its leaves, often growing under overhangs in nature. Gerard says *Primula allionii* also seems to relish this position. When plants on the spheres bloom, their flowers open like the sunrise moving across Earth in perhaps one of the world's most ingenious and novel public crevice gardens.

Armeria juniperifolia 'Drake's Deep Form' (left) makes a show as a group along with *Paronychia macedonica* on the right.

APEX

Crevices for Denver's dry climate

Denver's garden history has long been interwoven with rock gardening and perennial plant exploration. The city is also an epicenter for dry gardening because of limited local water supplies; in fact, the term 'xeriscape' was coined by its water bureaucracy. Influenced by its seat on the prairie but within eyeshot of the Rocky Mountains, Denver has its own garden style and plant palette.

The crevice garden was initiated by APEX, the Parks and Recreation department for the Denver suburb of Arvada. Wishing to beautify their newest sports complex with a cutting-edge amenity garden, they hired Kenton to design and build one for them. With the exception of Denver Botanic Gardens, there were no public crevice gardens in Denver at the time. Kenton consulted his mentors because he felt compelled to ensure his would be unique: it would be the first all-crevice, all-xeric public garden in Denver, using dryland plants but in the Czech style.

The garden used 55 tonnes (60 US tons) of Dakota formation sandstone in an area of 280sq m (3,000sq ft) built over several weeks and planted the following spring. Each of the five different mounds has its own soil mix, the tallest being nearly 2m (6ft) high with three layers of different soil inside. Gravel to match the stone could not be found locally, so a dump truck brought a load from 400km (250 miles) away. Kenton enlisted friend and co-author Paul, flying him down from Canada to help set rock and keep fresh eyes on this large project.

The garden was built from one side to the other, so that heavy equipment delivering loads of soil

and rock had access. The biggest mistake was the miscalculation of stone. The problem with a formula for tons per square foot (which works for a flat patio) is that it does not take into account an exponential increase in tonnage from the bulging height and volume of a mound! Kenton needed another 11 tonnes (12 US tons) to make up the difference.

With much aid from the Rocky Mountain Chapter of the North American Rock Garden Society, and many plants from local and distant growers, the garden was planted in the spring of 2015, starting with some 1,200 plants and 200 taxa. The design has many layers. It's often said that a mound looks out of place on a flat site, so Kenton sought inspiration from the scattered 'sky island' mountain ranges in the otherwise flat deserts of Arizona and Nevada. Repeating mounds were the key. However, while the

Rockies are visible in the distance from the garden, most of the immediate background to it is vertical human infrastructure of fence posts, a flagpole, light posts, and a church steeple, so Kenton used a few severely vertical conifers, *Juniperus scopulorum* 'Woodward', that would reconcile the garden with this backdrop without casting shade or leaves.

With plants, Kenton played it safe. He avoided maintenance and potential weed disasters by being brutally strict in the plant palette: no itchy or big cacti, no weedy reseeders, no aggressive rhizomes, and a strong limit to the number of herbaceous plants that require yearly clean-up. What plants are left after so many rules? A palette of native, Mediterranean, and dry-alpine cushions and buns. To soften the overwhelming hardness of the place, Kenton chose *Muhlenbergia reverchonii* as an ageless rugged grass to add life, movement, and translucence. Just a few dwarf conifers and manzanitas (*Arctostaphylos*) were used for greenness in the depth of freeze-dried winters, and for a little transition in size between towering junipers and petite bun plants.

Kenton resisted the urge to use fast, colorful filler plants while cushion plants slowly matured. It was only a year before the colorful blooms of *Acantholimon* species, *Moltkia petrea*, *Physaria ovatifolia*, *Phlox nana*, *Castilleja integra* and *Aloinopsis spathulata* appeared. This seasonal rainbow won the hearts of the regular users of the sports complex, who were at once introduced to the idea of crevice gardens and became protective of the garden. Children only occasionally damage plants by climbing the garden – a small price to pay for not having ugly barricades and signs.

The garden was christened with brutal temperature drops. The first winter killed off 20 percent of the plants, perhaps not hardy enough or not happy in their sites, but these were serendipitously replaced with seedlings of the survivors, revealing where plants preferred to be and which strains were truly hardy. This seemed to select more hardy strains of marginal plants such as *Aloinopsis*. Planted broadly, tender succulent species of *Agave* have survived best

on north aspects, perhaps because they prepare sooner for winter cold and stay asleep instead of being fooled awake then killed by frost. Bulbs, with their shallow roots, generally dislike the lean and dry surface soils of the garden.

There is no maintenance budget, so the garden goes without plant labels. Overhead irrigation every two weeks may play the biggest part in minimizing weeds. The few weeds prefer the bases of the mounds, where slightly more aggressive plants such as *Zauschneria* and *Stachys lavandulifolia* can repel them.

While it was a great deal of work to create, the APEX garden requires minimal maintenance and provides strong yearly dividends. It continues to function as a bank of mother plants for local propagators and as a seed factory for uncommon plants such as *Acantholimon halophilum*. With the quirky pop of pickleball games ever in the background, it hits an unlikely sweet spot between low input and a strong collection of special plants.

Opposite: One of the five mounds that make up this immersive public garden.

Top: The golden *Physaria ovalifolia* is a showstopping but short-lived reseeder that plays a seasonal supporting role for standalone specimens.

Left: A weed-resistant design keeps maintenance down to about 15 hours per year and biodiversity ensures flowering for most of the season.

Domenique Turnbull
Classic and new

Some rock gardeners are lucky enough to enjoy the coolness, daytime temperature swings, and more regular precipitation that comes with gardening in the mountains themselves. One of these is Domenique Turnbull, who lives outside Colorado Springs, beside the road that winds to the top of the famous Pike's Peak on a decidedly gritty granitic soil.

Dom is a rock gardener of German descent who learned the skill from his mother. His European approach shows up in his resistance to simply buying rock like most Americans do; instead, he favors scavenging it, which means meeting interesting people, taking scenic day trips, getting good exercise, but, most importantly, being able to hand-choose every single stone. He also found that his locally available roadbase provides a good mix of gritty, gravelly aggregate and mineral fines to provide elemental nutrients to his alpine plants. He makes his own hypertufa planters, and likes how different troughs allow him to use a different stone in each, since mixed stones look strange in the rock garden itself. One of Dom's most exciting innovations came from his love affair with rounded, white-marbled stones which he hand-picked from a mixed pile of actual glacial till. These heavy, metamorphic gneiss dumplings shine with ancient polishing, revealing vibrating lines of white.

Round stones don't allow for the highest construction, and are mostly not used in crevice gardens because of ingrained conventions. This was not a problem for Dom; a few big, round rocks made his garden plenty tall. He set them close together, creating crevices that are not linear but triangular and starfish-shaped. He plants by digging from the wide open side of these wedge-shaped gaps, nestling in new plants like happy pickles in a tight rock hamburger bun. The arrangement is garnished with hand-collected gravel of the same material in varying sizes.

Careful observers will realize that, in a nod to the Czech style, Domenique has oriented the marbled striations in his rock with one another. They give an intuitive organization with an aesthetic novelty that only a geologist would realize would never happen in nature. By breaking the rules, Dom found a new option for arranging special stones.

This permanent glimmering backdrop of stone shows off a seasonally dynamic rainbow cast of cool-blooded gentians, *Douglasia, Primula, Androsace,* and whatever new and rare taxa interests Dom at the time, all of which enjoy excellent surface drainage, a nice dry surface, and a deep, moist root-run.

In the drabness of winter, the rocks and their shadows shine, opposite, while in spring and summer, top, deep greens are set off like rich bezels that feature colored gems like *Androsace alpina*, above, which prospers in the irregular crevices.

Growing without limits in Prague

On a garden tour, upon seeing a rare plant in a garden, you'll often hear a visitor say something like, 'Ah, that's so rare, but all the Czechs are growing it.' The Czech Rock Garden Society, based in Prague, is one of the greatest strongholds of rock garden culture on Earth, often the benchmark for quality of growership by home gardeners. Here, there seems to be no clear distinction between a rock garden and a crevice garden – if you have a rock garden it is probably a crevice garden. Jiří is a member of this club.

His family's house is on a fairly flat suburban lot, and wrapped around it are a varied array of growing systems for saxatile plants. There are nearly traditional perennial beds, raised peat beds, concrete troughs, an alpine house, a 'tufa tunnel', rock gardens built like mountains from flat ground, and a rock garden built on one of his only natural slopes. Jiří has crevices in all of these environments. To supply these gardens, he grows many of his own plants in a small shaded home nursery along a fence, started as seed or cuttings in an alpine house.

His rear crevice gardens are nearly as tall as a person, rising from the flat ground. This artificial topography increases his plantable surface area and creates varied sun aspects and drainage situations. This series of crevice gardens weaves in and out of concrete troughs, creating both extremely deep root-runs to the ground as well as pockets where plants are limited. Dark-colored stone gathers heat in the daytime. Here, gentians savor shady north and east pockets, *Arenaria* enjoy high, dry crevices,

Centaurea bake on sunny slopes, and dwarf conifers add evergreen structure throughout. His paths are gravel, and the less picky growers seed into it, leaving the choice real estate for the more rare and difficult plants.

Even his raised beds with woody plants in them are playfully mixed with crevices. Pale wall rock undulates into crevice features, so that instead of an ordinary stone wall, he has a garden unto itself with plants teeming from the cracks. This creates another suite of microclimates with sun-reflecting light-colored stone as well as crevices with access to the rich soil inside the raised bed. This certainly gives him a huge choice of planting spaces to choose from when he has a new plant to place.

The tufa tunnel is roofed with clear polycarbonate to prevent rain from wetting the rock garden inside, giving Jiří total control over irrigation and allowing him to grow plants from drier places than Prague, especially a collection of *Dionysia*, challenging *Campanula*, gesneriads, and *Daphne*. All of the stone within is porous tufa, so he can grow plants not only in the cracks but directly in the stone.

Jiří is a diehard plant lover. Visitors are amazed, and tell him he is a magician for growing all of the rarest, most sought-after 'Holy Grail' plants, but it is not magic that he uses to get it done. He is fascinated by the variety of saxatile plants and the challenge of growing them, and he is willing to make the time, effort, and expense to painstakingly create the environments they need. Jiří does not limit himself with what he is willing to build to accommodate

plants. What he has found is that crevices are the most basic, if most universal, strategy for growing saxatile plants, and he mixes them with other tools to grow everything he wants.

Jiří Papoušek has a thing for buns, opposite, and like most Czechs, is not snobbish about growing *Sempervivum* (above). His tufa-creviced tunnel, below, is where the rarest gems are stored.

Success with the diagonal

Gardeners and wanderers of the American West are spoiled with constant vistas of rocky places, many of them mesas formed by exposed sedimentary stone, many of which host saxatile plants. Here, very few strata are forced completely vertical; most are flat or gently diagonal. This type of geology is very familiar to Westerners, so, for many, vertical crevice gardens have never resonated with them as natural.

John Lawyer is one such Westerner in Colorado Springs. His backyard crevice garden covers most of the space, with a main diagonal path bisecting it and creating different aspects on the mounds that flank it. The path is paved with stone seamlessly and irregularly, so there is no clear boundary between path and garden. Plants spring from every crack between stones, which, most notably, are diagonally tilted; his rocks all touch one another, leaning upon their neighbors. The whole garden is generally oriented to the same tilt, within a few degrees. The irregular shape of the stones as well as open pockets create spaces for his plants between secure and stable stones. By allowing the stones to support one another as well as keeping crevices open, John has succeeded in creating something that looks more natural to him but still works to grow plants.

The warm, rusty seams of stone underpin the wild-west color scheme that unifies Western American plants: bright green *Yucca harrimaniae*, cool silver *Artemisia*, and ruddy *Eriogonum*. In June appears the hot flash of native but garden-elusive *Castilleja integra*.

As for that slightly deviating orientation? He certainly didn't use a compass, but insisted on doing it by eye and without a strict line: 'As irregular as possible!' he says. A massive secret to achieving naturalism is that the tilted axis of the stone appears to dive underground from whence it came, where it is apparently subsumed by soil. He says the inspiration for his formula came entirely from studying nature. Looking at his garden, we believe him.

There's room for big plants such as *Yucca harrimaniae*, opposite, and hardy *Cylindropuntia* aff. *whipplei* 'Snow Leopard', above, as well as small like *Draba aizoides*, right.

Juniper Level Botanic Garden

Humid crevice gardening

Plant Delights Nursery in Raleigh, North Carolina, is a beloved American mail order nursery that celebrates unfettered plant lust, specializing in exotics from hardy orchids and palm trees to hostas. The brainchild of Tony Avent, plantsman extraordinaire, Plant Delights grows and offers a staggering list of perennials, the result of the nursery's own explorations, plant trials, breeding, selection, and propagation. But the nursery also operates as the progenitor and financial support system for the adjacent and intertwined Juniper Level Botanic Garden, an 11-hectare (28-acre) site that hosts a remarkable 28,000 taxa of plants.

It is no surprise that such a church of plant worshippers would experiment with crevice gardens. Their first trial beds were only the second crevice gardens ever known in the American Southeast. The choice of material solved the problem of the concrete foundation of an old house and parking pad razed on the property; the nursery owners took this burden and converted it into gold. After favorable results with their large crevice garden trial beds, they hired Kenton to help flesh out and strategize for a giant crevice garden – probably the largest on Earth. With only a week of coaching from Kenton, Juniper Level's research and grounds supervisor, Jeremy Schmidt, exploded the plan into a gargantuan garden: a 122m (400ft) long feature which used up well over 181 tonnes (178 US tons) of recycled concrete armoring a formerly precarious unsupported slope. Jeremy built in a dizzying variety of specialized microclimates and features such as alkaline and acid seeps to home some very esoteric plants. He engineered a soil

medium for the garden of which the main component is a manufactured expanded slate called PermaTill, originally a local cinder block byproduct. It offers very high nutrient and water retention as well as unusually high air penetration. One surprise lesson was learned during a long cold winter period in which normally hardy plants froze to death overnight. Autopsied victims showed that the unusually generous air spaces of their soil mix allowed cold to penetrate the soil much more deeply than usual.

The concrete breaks any rules of strict geologic orientation, because concrete is not geology. Its form bends to the landscape, plants, and path, sometimes curling, twisting, and running into itself in perpendicular joints. All of this variety is brought together by it being one dominating and unifying material, as well as a consistent dark gravel top-dressing, allowing any future additions of the garden to get away with anything aesthetically. The stark contrast between the top-dressing and the concrete chunks is enforced and enjoyed, rather than hidden as it would be for a naturalistic design. The rusted impression of reinforcing wire in the concrete is left to show here and there, revealing rather than hiding the history of the concrete. During construction, Jeremy and Kenton came back to the site to find that, overnight, Tony Avent had installed some very sculptural standing dead cypress from the property into the slope, shoring up the notion of a post-apocalyptic garden: bright, exotic, active plants seem to burst from the seams of the ruins of a bygone city. Jeremy took full advantage of the artistic freedom in using concrete for crevice gardening, exploring new possibilities and later applying his talents as a 'rock stacker' outside of his work at the botanical garden.

The team at Juniper Level have continued to find that more and more species that are easily grown in drier places but have previously failed in North Carolina will thrive in their crevice garden. Bright arilbred iris effortlessly pop from the garden with their dark eyes, succulents mash themselves between the slabs, and Mediterranean herbs spread and weave between the lines. A gallery of agaves perch on the garden at a rare eye-level vantage point, a nod to the cliff-dwelling origins of many species.

Juniper Level boldly led the way with their Urbanite Outfitters crevice garden exhibit, even gaining the attention of the *Washington Post*, which put crevice gardens onto the national public stage. We expect that future years of JLBG's diligent testing and observation will stoke a growing interest in crevice gardens in the humid Southeastern USA and well beyond.

Above: The crevice garden proper in progress. Making its own rules, it has novel curves highlighted by darker mulch.
Below: Even a drone can see something special about the first crevice garden trial built at Juniper Level Botanic Garden.

Next pages: Mediterranean and other xeric plants previously ungrowable at JLBG are the proof of the pudding.

Denver Botanic Gardens
Masonry crevices

The Rock and Alpine Garden at Denver Botanic Gardens is already well established on the map of influential rock gardens in the world. It served locally as a hub for new perennial plant material, connecting locals to the international gardening community, and then reciprocated to the world by sharing its own style and cultivated native plants, greatly driven by Panayoti Kelaidis. It continues to be a major player in a time when the state of Colorado is forming its own gardening culture in the dry, cold-winter continental climate of the 'Mile-High City'.

The Denver area has been a hot spot for rock gardening since at least the 1980s and became a crevice garden hot spot in the 2000s when Mike Kintgen, curator of alpine collections, began to build them in the gardens to highlight the saxatile collections. DBG's exhibits proved that crevice gardens are not just a foreign novelty but also a useful and aesthetically legitimate planting strategy in the dry interior western USA. One of the most popular new exhibits at Denver Botanic is the 'Steppe Garden', which educates the public about the world-wide steppe biome in which Denver sits.

The Steppe Garden's separate beds are dedicated to continents where steppe occurs and the plants that grow there. Then there are two curious freestanding features: large, sandstone obelisks created by mason Thad Wojdyla. These exhibits are rounded in form, perhaps akin to upturned boat hulls, inspired by bun and cushion plants. Their surfaces are composed of slivers of mortared sandstone that have very thin spaces between them for true chasmophytes. The

The seminal crevice garden, above, at Denver Botanic Garden would fuel confidence for the later, more experimental Steppe Garden, opposite and below.

sandstone plates were set in place with wads of mortar onto a cinder-block core in the structures' centers. The medium that the chasmophytes are growing in is a novel slurry of clay, potting mix, and seeds which was extruded into the gaps like cake icing, engineered by the associate director of horticulture and curator of steppe collections, Michael Bone. He followed tradition and planted small rooted cuttings into this fresh slurry. Unsurprisingly, true chasmophytes have been the most successful plants, such as the very woolly *Verbascum wiedemannianum*, silver *Arctotis adpressa*, and waxy *Iberis simplex*. American rock-loving *Heuchera abramsii* and *H. sanguinea* are growing slowly and steadily, keeping much smaller leaves than they normally do in open gardens. Africa is represented by *Delosperma lavisiae*, and there has been reseeding of Mongolian *Orostachys spinosa*.

Historically, the approach to crevice garden construction has been simply setting rocks in soil and mortar has not been used to keep stones in place. The obelisks, however, approach crevices as masonry, starting with a structure and opening it up to be plantable. This represents a whole new world of growing plants between rocks, stretching and blurring the very definition of a crevice garden. The steppe obelisks are most different in that there is

not a core of pure earth inside, like the base mound within traditional crevice gardens. Instead, they have a network of soil woven between the permeable sandstone, which may actually be a more accurate representation of cracking and crumbling rock features in nature.

Alan Furness

Design for beauty and maintenance

A prolific rock gardener over many years, Alan Furness is known on the show benches in the UK for potted alpines. He is also a cutting-edge grower and popularizer of the genus *Celmisia* at his home garden situated in the beautiful Northumbrian countryside.

Alan was one of the four people in the working group who installed the crevice garden at the Alpine Garden Society's address in Pershore under the direction of Zdeněk Zvolánek. As well as the ability to grow choice plants, the geologically informed rules of crevice garden construction attracted this retired geography teacher, so he built several of his own crevice gardens at home, inspired by local sandstone anticlines. He is mindful about repeating angles of edges of stones, and lining up faces for good distances – but not too much, finding a believable and natural balance between harmony and variety of line and form. Alan's solid-looking designs are thanks to strict adherence to rules – consistent angle of dip, direction of strike, and thickness of strata. On steep tiny cliffs where soil must be contained, his sandstones are tight together, while more level surfaces are left more open and filled simply with sifted local soil that supports self-sowing colonies of *Androsace laggeri*, *Potentilla ancistrifolia* var. *dickinsii*, *Dianthus microlepis* and *Callianthemum anemonoides*. *Draba dedeana* also completely fills crevices and excludes weeds, reducing maintenance as he intended. *Daphne x hendersonii* thrives, if becoming a bit large for his tastes. All enjoy the deeply buried stone that gives them exclusive root-runs despite being not very high off the ground.

Alan's low-lying crevice beds are ringed with gravel mulch to separate them from turf grass, provide access, and create a semi-formal connection between traditional lawn and naturalistic rock features, looking not unlike maps or dioramas laid out on his lawn. There and elsewhere in his garden he employs deep gravel mulch to dissuade weed seedlings, while all the inviting, fertile, or plantable spots are crammed with locally adapted plants, allowing him to preside over more gardens and more beautiful plants manageably.

Opposite: Alan Furness's crevice on the lawn, above, resembles a map of our planet with rocky continents where *Daphne x hendersonii* 'Fritz Kummert', below, savours the tight root-run.

PLANT PROFILES

There is no such thing as a complete list of all crevice-worthy plants, since the possibilities are constantly being refreshed. Species that have failed for a gardener in other situations can be tried again in a crevice, and new species or selections, even plants new to science, are brought into cultivation every year. Some previously 'ungrowable' groups have been tamed over time with selective breeding, and this will only continue in the future, widening our plant palette.

Tetraneuris scaposa syn. *Hymenoxys scaposa* in the foreground of seed collector Vladimir Staněk's crevice garden.

The crevice plant suite is not restricted to mounds, carpets, and buns, but also includes different plant forms such as geophytes (bulbs), lignaceous (woody) plants, graminoids (grass and grass-like plants), and forbs (herbaceous plants that are not grass). Most crevice plants are, of course, miniatures, and not all require a crevice to thrive. Dwarf conifers exemplify this because they are easily grown in the open garden but are an appropriate scale and form for a crevice garden. All other factors being equal, size is the final limiting factor for a plant's appropriateness and appeal in a crevice garden, so the species mentioned below are almost always the smallest of their respective genus – though of course larger crevice gardens and larger rocks can warrant larger plants. All plants listed are perennial.

Many of the following plants not only benefit from crevice life, but require it to grow in a certain climate, or anywhere at all. They include taxa that can be grown easily in most temperate climates, as well as a few that are pickier. The selection here is intended to be a starting point for new crevice gardeners, a reference for those shopping for what's available, and a checklist for those diversifying their collection. It includes taxa that are popular in modern rock gardens as well as some that are new, rare, or difficult. However, consulting with nearby friends and making your own experiments are the only ways to know what is possible in your own garden. So many great discoveries of possibility are made by those who 'didn't know better'.

Individual plants grown from the same batch of seed can vary in height, form, and color, but here we list averages. Measurements are given as height by width (H x W).

We use a gardener's taxonomy (rather than a botanist's), since scientific nomenclature is currently changing fast. Rock gardeners tend to gravitate toward scientific names rather than common ones and many plants in this list do not even have a common name. We include them when they do and are in common use. Plant families are provided to draw some connection to their better-known relatives outside the crevice garden. Information on a plant's origin is given to shed light on its needs, as well as general observations on culture, propagation, and use.

'. . . where mountains are crumbled into ghastly slopes of shattered rock . . . they [the flowers] brilliantly spring from nature's ruined battleground, as if the mother of earth had sent up her sweetest and loveliest children to plead with the forces of destruction.'

William Robinson, *Alpine Plants for English Gardens*, 1870

Acantholimon trojanum in seed.

Acantholimon hedinii

Hardiness

We list the hardiness for plants on an individual basis, following each species named in the text. For many of the plants on this list, the limiting factor in being able to grow them is not the cold, so hardiness ratings are not the only key to successful cultivation, but a general rule of thumb. Numbers are not gospel. Most of these plants can withstand greater cold than seen by most temperate garden situations because they are alpine or montane. Equally critical survival factors are summer heat and drying, winter moisture/humidity, and adequate drainage during dormancy. The protective insulation of snow cover can increase winter cold survival. Not all Mediterranean plants may be hardy in the coldest climate zones. Also, a plant with potential to be bone-hardy may suffer in a local climate where temperature change happens fast, such as sudden frosts, for which the plant is not prepared. To further complicate matters, there is often hardiness variability within the species.

Top: *Penstemon rupicola alba*
Bottom: *Aethionema subulatum*

ACANTHOLIMON
PRICKLY THRIFT

Family	Plumbaginaceae
General habit	Mounded evergreen buns or mats, steppe to alpine,
Origin	Mediterranean to the Tien Shan
Garden needs	Full sun, dry

The painfully pointed leaves of this genus, held in congested rosettes, come together to create perfectly symmetrical domes in youth (3–5 years) which later expand amorphously to engulf significant space in the crevice garden, some of them reaching up to 60cm (2ft) across and 30cm (12in) tall. Nearly all bloom in various shades of pink, and feature ornamental papery 'seed parachute' calyxes afterward. Most can be grown from cuttings. They are notorious for rarely producing viable seed in gardens, but wild-harvested seed germinates readily. Classic *A. venustum* (Z5), **top**, offers coarse, larger, grayish-green spheres under arched sprays of large, hot pink blooms in summer. *A. ulicinum* (Z5) is similar in form but features shorter spikes of light-pink flowers over bluish-green foliage. *A. trojanum* (Z5), **middle**, may be the most broadly growable, offering unique dark green foliage and flowers that barely rise above the bun. *A. bracteatum ssp. capitatum* (Z6) is grown for its blue-green foliage and pink flower 'heads' as the name suggests. *A. hedinii* (Z3) and *A. tianshanicum* (Z4) are some of the smallest at 2.5 x 5cm (1 x 2in), growing extra slowly with flowers virtually embedded in the buns. Kenton's favorite is the softball-sized, gentle dark green globe, *A. puberulum* ssp. *longiscapum* (Z4), with flowers atop thready stems. Ger van den Beuken says the best is *A. saxifragiforme* (Z4), **bottom**, also a small ball, but of blue starfish stuck with thick pink flower stems.

184

AETHIONEMA
STONECRESS

Family	Brassicaceae
General habit	Semi-shrubby perennials
Origin	Europe and West Asia, particularly Turkey
Garden needs	Full sun, dry

The word *Aethionema* means 'to kindle or brighten', which these plants certainly do when grown among the rocks. Most are easy and reliable to cultivate and self-sow into colonies after a few years. Their powdery blue-green foliage looks great in winter after the flower stems have been removed. The most famous garden species is *A.* 'Warley Rose', but it is too large for most crevices. We rely upon the dainty *A. subulatum* (Z3), **top**, *A. schistosum* (Z3) and *A. kotschyi* (Z7), **bottom**, which reach only 5cm (2in).

ALOINOPSIS

HARDY LIVING STONE

Family	Aizoaceae
General habit	Succulent buns
Origin	South Africa
Garden needs	Full sun, dry

Despite their tropical appearance, a few *Aloinopsis* species have been known to survive Z5 winters when kept dry. Their succulent, spoon-shaped leaves form hard buns just above ground level. Spring flowers open flat with sunshine, revealing gorgeous, shimmering daisies. The hardiest two species are *A. spathulata* (Z5b), growing to 5 x 20cm (2 x 8in), with pale to burning pink flowers. The smaller, slightly less hardy but no less beautiful *A. acuta* (Z6) has cupped-triangular leaves and white-eyed yellow flowers. These two hardy species have parented intergeneric hybrids with at least a half-dozen related genera, yielding flowers in a veritable rainbow of brights to pastels, two-tones, stripes, and even evening or night blooms. They mature quickly from seed or cuttings. *Aloinopsis spathulata* hybrid, **top**, and *Aloinopsis/Nananthus* hybrid, **bottom**.

ANDROSACE

ROCK JASMINE

Family	Primulaceae
General habit	Lax mats to densely congested cushions
Origin	Mountains of the Northern Hemisphere
Garden needs	Sun, regular water

Grow these diminutive alpines in sun and gritty soil, avoiding summer dryness and winter wet. *A. villosa* (Z3), **top**, is a variable species from limestone in the European mountains which forms a small hairy mat of gray-green leaves beneath flowers of white to pink with a reddish eye. *A. carnea* (Z3) makes small, tight domes with pink to white flowers. *A. muscoidea* (Z5) is a stoloniferous mat from Pakistan boasting silver-green foliage and stemless white flowers that turn lavender after pollination. *A. vitaliana* (Z3), **bottom**, is the new name for long-loved *Vitaliana primuliflora,* whose primrose-yellow flowers are held tightly to a tuft of narrow silver leaves. An honorable mention goes to *A. barbulata* (Z5) for its pure white flowers and tiny woolly rosettes.

ANTHEMIS CRETICA

MAT DAISY, CHAMOMILE

Family	Asteraceae
General habit	Evergreen mats
Origin	Mediterranean/Near East
Garden needs	Sun, dry

A. cretica (Z4), **left**, from dry montane to alpine habitats, is a highly variable but compact woody mat of gray or green leaves with ascending stems supporting classic snow-white, yellow-eyed daisies. Only 10cm (4in) high and easy from seed, its variety of form from at least twenty-five subspecies can be enjoyed.

AQUILEGIA
COLUMBINE

Family	Ranunculaceae
General habit	Dwarf forbs
Origin	Northern Hemisphere
Garden needs	Sun/part shade, moist soil

Alpines of dwarf stature and often large flowers entice the crevice gardener. They are easily grown from seed but highly promiscuous – don't count on pure forms from garden-collected seed. The stand-by *A. flabellata* 'Nana' (Z3), **bottom**, from Japan and Korea, features substantial bicolor (usually blue and white) flowers standing 5–15cm (2–6in) just above the foliage. *A. saximontana* (Z3) is a narrow endemic to Colorado's Rockies, at 5–25cm (2–10in) very variable in height, with slightly smaller flowers held just over the soft foliage. The elusive queen of the genus is *A. jonesii* (Z2) (Jones's columbine), **top**, a tiny cushion of clefted leaves which grows strictly on high limestone areas in the middle Rockies. The large, pure purple flowers are endlessly sought and rarely enjoyed in cultivation. Pastel *A. laramiensis* (Z3) and the soft red and gold *A. grahamii* (Z3) are easier petite charmers for the collector.

ARENARIA
SANDWORT

Family	Caryophyllaceae
General habit	Tight buns
Origin	Northern Hemisphere mountains
Garden needs	Sun, regular water

Named from the Latin for sand, these plants seem adaptable in any well-drained garden soil in full sun or afternoon shade in hot climates. The best form dense buns so hard they resemble living rocks. In most species, the minuscule white flowers are secondary to form. Classic *A. alfacarensis* (Z5) is a mounding, hard, hummock of a plant in soil or tufa. *A. tetraquetra* (Z5) is essentially a coarser version. *A. ex. Wallowa Mountains* (Z3), **left**, is always a mossy, green crowd-pleaser that resembles a small version of Greek *A. stellata*. Honorable mention goes to rock-referencing *A. lithops* (Z4). None reach more than 7.5cm (3in).

ARMERIA
THRIFT, SEA THRIFT

Family	Caryophyllaceae
General habit	Tight buns
Origin	Northern Hemisphere mountains
Garden needs	Sun, regular water

So easy to grow from cuttings, thrifts can be found as bedding plants and in florist shops. Most are tufts of soft grassy or needle-like leaves with pink pom-pom flower heads on stems of varying height. The most common in rock gardens is *A. maritima* (Z3). As the seaside name suggests, it is highly tolerant of saline environments. A surprising disjunct population occurs in the Rockies of Colorado and Utah, *A. maritima* subp. *sibirica*. It features pink or white flowers 20cm (8in) high, spreading slowly to 30cm (12in). *A. juniperifolia* (Z3), **left**, known as the Spanish thrift, is a choice little plant reaching 8 x 13cm (3 x 5in) with soft pink flowers held closely against needle-like leaves. Finally, seek out the mountain thrift *A. alpina* (Z4). All require decent drainage and bright sun.

ASPERULA
ALPINE WOODRUFF

Family	Rubiaceae
General habit	Tight to loose mats
Origin	Mediterranean mountains
Garden needs	Sun, regular water

A favorite of the passerby, *Asperula* has pointed but soft leaves and forms tight, slowly spreading micro-carpets less than 2.5cm (1in) tall. The plants creep around corners to highlight crevices, covered with tiny pink upward-facing flowers. Plant these high where they will have perfect drainage and avoid winter wet and high summer humidity. The easy and somewhat xeric *A. boissieri* (Z4) is blueish-leaved. We recommend the green-leaved Sicilian *A. gussonei* (Z3) and *A. nitida* (Z4) from Greece and Turkey. These are similar, with tiny trumpets of varying shades of pink. Honorable mention goes to *A. sintenisii (Z3),* **left**. All are relatively easy from seed and easier from division.

ASTRAGALUS
MILK VETCH

Family	Fabaceae
General habit	Dwarf shrubs, forbs, and buns
Origin	Almost world-wide
Garden needs	Full sun, dry

While many species of this massive genus are tall herbs and shrubs, there are a good number of these tap-rooted beasts that qualify for our purposes with their showy pea-style flowers, most of which hail from alpine and steppe environments. A classic is the white-flowered but purple-keeled *A. angustifolius* (Z4), **bottom**. It forms long-lived and sizable low spiny shrubs. Difficult, smaller, but more desirably shaped are *A. spatulatus* (Z3), **top,** and *A. simplicifolius* (Z3), from west-central North America, which are small silver buns or tufts with pea-shaped flowers perched on tiny stems. *A. utahensis* (Z4), from the Wasatch Mountains, features bright pink flowers on woolly white plants reaching 15 x 46cm (6 x 18in). The elusive holy grail species *A. coccineus* is a carmine-red version. Many species have ornate seedpods which are often essential for identification.

AZORELLA (SYN. BOLAX)
PLASTIC PLANT, LLARETA

Family	Apiaceae
General habit	Ground-hugging hard carpet/ buns
Origin	South America, from
Garden needs	seacoasts to high alpine areas Sun, regular water, tolerates maritime exposures

The genus *Azorella* features a couple of species for us. The easiest and most available is *A. trifurcata* (Z4), **left**, with hard, finely divided, glossy green leaves that have earned it the nickname 'plastic plant', feeling every bit like first-generation plastic AstroTurf. The summer blooms are tiny yellow umbels. In gardens it rarely mounds up more than 12cm high (5in) but will form a large, spreading ground cover in mellow climates; it is nearly always grown from division. *A. compacta* (Z8) is rarer and slower in cultivation, and in the Andes is the famous 'llareta', growing into ancient, acid-green cushions.

The brooms

Family	Fabaceae
General habit	Tight to loose mats
Origin	Mediterranean mountains
Garden needs	Sun, dry

Some diminutive brooms with their flashy pea-like flowers have earned a place in rock gardens. From dry, stony places, they are drought tolerant, with wiry rock-hugging stems. Most are warm gold, with some wonderful exceptions. Consider the following four, all different genera: *Cytisus hirsutus* var. *demissus* (Z5) is a prunable large mat 5cm (2in) tall with hairy deciduous leaves; the reliable *Genista lydia* var. *lydia* (Z5), **top**, is a tiny shrub 2.5 x 46cm (1 x 18in) with bright golden flowers. *Chamaecytisus pygmaeus* (Z6) is a real charmer and the classiest mentioned here: finer leaves and growing only 2.5cm (1in) high! *Erinacea anthyllis* (Z5b), **right**, however, forms an ultimately creeping dome about 46cm (18in) tall, built of rigid if invisible spikes, but earning its keep with novel lavender-blue flowers. Collecting seeds can result in bloodshed.

Anti-clockwise from top left:
*Allium crenulatum; Tulipa
sogdiana; Rhodohypoxis
baurii; Crocus cancellatus;
Cyclamen coum*

Bulbs and rhizomes

Unless a crevice garden is very large, big classic bulbs won't be among the repertoire, but dwarf bulbs are often grown in open soil pockets or miniature meadows adjacent to a crevice garden where they can naturalize without becoming weedy. However, we can also employ the crevice garden to grow bulbs that are challenged by our climate. The body of the bulb, corm, tuber, or rhizome enjoys the drainage and clean media while its deeper roots can seek moisture and nutrients. This is especially useful if you want to grow bulbs from dryer places in a wet climate. A crevice can also help tender bulbs or rhizomes warm up and/or dry to ripen and harden for winter. Common genera include the smaller *Acis, Allium, Anemone, Brodiaea, Bulbocodium, Chionodoxa, Crocus, Cyclamen, Eranthis, Gagea, Galanthus, Iris, Narcissus, Rhodohypoxis, Romulea,* and *Tulipa.*

CAMPANULA
BELLFLOWER, HAREBELL

Family	Campanulaceae
General habit	Dwarf forbs
Origin	Northern Hemisphere
Garden needs	Sunny, regular water, often calcareous soil

No crevice garden is complete without examples of *Campanula* (the Latin name meaning 'little bell'). The genus includes a plethora of diminutive species that suit rockeries because they are often found in crevices in nature. It is painful to list so few here. *C. cochlearifolia* (Z3), from the European Alps, has tiny glossy green leaves and miniature pendant blue or white bells on stems just 7.5cm (3in) high. Its thin roots will spread underground, sometimes strongly, along the length of even the tightest crevice. *C. raineri* (Z3), from Italy, is a choice clump with disproportionately large, upturned flowers on stemless leaves. This dry-crevice trio from Turkey and nearby have elegantly dangling stems of herbaceous, toothed foliage: *C. choruhensis* (Z3), *C. betulifolia* (Z3), and *C. troegerae* (Z3), **bottom**, distinguished mostly by their less- or more-flared flowers of pink-flushed white. *C. zoysii* syn. *Favratia zoysii* (Z6) is a chasmophyte with crowded leaves supporting its light blue, strangely puckered flowers. Finally, the beautiful *C. waldsteiniana* (Z5), **top**, will stop you in your tracks as a hemispherical mound completely blue with outward-facing 'satellite dishes'.

CASTILLEJA
PAINTBRUSH

Family	Orobanchaceae
General habit	Forbs
Origin	Mainly North America
Garden needs	Full sun/part shade, dry

A unique genus luring plant-lovers with striking colors from white, yellow, and orange to scarlet red, *Castilleja* species are in a class all their own. They are hemi-parasitic, meaning they naturally grow by partially freeloading from a host plant. Some knowledge of their physiology is needed to grow them successfully. While they can parasitize plants completely foreign to them, they do much better with certain other local genera with similar garden needs. These are often *Bouteloua, Festuca, Artemisia, Eriogonum,* and *Penstemon*. The seeds need cold stratification or gibberellic acid treatment to germinate. Sow them alone, fertilize them well, and prick them to pair with a host, planting them then or after they've attached to the host. Pruning their tops often helps in transplanting. *Castilleja integra* (Z4), **top**, has proven itself as the easiest species in dry continental climates for crevice gardens. *C. miniata* (Z3), *C. coccinea* (Z3), and *C. applegatei* (Z6) are more growable in wetter climates. *C. sessiliflora* is easy and long-lived but with humble green to rosy blooms. *C. scabrida* (Z4), **bottom**, a natural crevice-dweller known as the 'rimrock paintbrush', is a challenge for the masters. Its lacy, compact, 10cm (4in) tall blooms of fiery embers appear with hardly any leaves at all.

CENTAUREA
CORNFLOWER

Family	Asteraceae
General habit	Small thistle-like forbs
Origin	Mostly Northern Hemisphere
	Mediterranean and steppe
Garden needs	Full sun, dry

As thistles and knapweeds, many within the genus are terrible nuisances, yet a handful of dwarfs from dry Eurasia grace the crevice. Their fascinating architecture is centered around pineapple-like flower heads, gilded with ornate phyllaries supporting colorful petals. *C. drabifolia* (Z4), ***top***, and *C. pestalozzae* (Z3) have golden-yellow and slightly spined flowers on unarmed plants, with a range of leaf form and color, 8 x 30cm (3 x 12in). Similar dusty-leafed *C. pindicola* (Z5) has white cosmic flowers and dark accents. *C. montis-borlae* (Z3), ***bottom***, 6 x 20cm (2½ x 8in), is an endangered endemic of marble crevices in Italy's Apuan Alps. Easily cultivated, its soft magenta flowers look like classic garden bachelor's buttons but on flat, red-stemmed plants with dark green felted leaves.

Left: *Castilleja integra*
Right top: *Centaurea pestalozzae*
Right bottom: *Campanula raineri*

Conifers

Some say that dwarf conifers form the backbone of the rock garden. They are the stoic sentinels, growing slowly and timelessly anchored so that they remain seemingly unchanged through the years but stand out in winter. An array of forms and foliage colors in a suite of genera await the collector – through green globes, pendulous mops, blue spires, and golden carpets, you can have a year-round garden of conifers alone! Be sure to choose the best varieties that remain dwarf for many years and require little or no pruning. Conifers can be thinned and crown-raised to transform them into miniature trees, each with its own unique character. The following are selections for the crevice garden:

- *Abies lasiocarpa* 'Duflon' (Z2) (subalpine fir), 46 x 46cm (18 x 18in), from the Olympic Mountains, USA is possibly the choicest of all dwarf conifers creating the tightest symmetrical sphere.
- *Chamaecyparis obtusa* (false cedar): 'Juniperoides' (Z5), 10 x 10cm (4 x 4in); 'Minima' (Z5), 25 x 25cm (10 x 10in); 'Hage' (Z5), 40 x 25cm (16 x 10in). All form miniature stately mounds whose needles are arranged in fan-shaped swirls.
- *Cryptomeria japonica* (Japanese cedar) 'Tanzu' (Z6), 15 x 15cm (6 x 6in); 'Tenzan' (Z7), 15 x 13cm (6 x 5in). They feature light green spiky foliage which may bronze in winter. 'Tanzu' grows slowly to form an irregular pyramid while 'Tenzan' becomes a symmetrical cushion slightly wider than tall.
- *Juniperus communis* 'Compressa' (Z4) (juniper): a timeless classic – plant together for instant groves of blue spires. The smallest cultivars of *J. communis* reach a maximum 50cm (20in) high. *J. horizontalis* 'Blue Pygmy' (Z3) is a globose shrub reaching 12 x 25cm (5 x 10in).
- *Picea abies* 'Little Gem' (Z3) (Norway spruce): there are many variants, the smallest reaching 30 x 45cm (12 x 18in).
- *Picea glauca* var. *albertiana* 'Pixie Dust' (Z3): dwarf Alberta spruce is a conical plant to 38 x 15cm (15 x 6in).
- *Pinus mugo*: Any miniature mugo pine, such as 'Mitsch Mini' (Z3), which reaches 15 x 15cm (6 x 6in) in 10 years.

Above: Growing very slowly, and living for many years, *Juniperus communis* 'Compressa', (left, upright), *Picea abies* 'Little Gem' (light green, left middle), and *Picea glauca* 'Pixie Dust' (upright, right) are all perfect selections for the crevice garden.
Right: *Picea glauca* var. *albertiana* 'Pixie Dust'

CONVOLVULUS
MORNING GLORY

Family	Convolvulaceae
General habit	Woody-stemmed buns
Origin	Mediterranean regions
Garden needs	Full sun, dry

Despite their weed relatives, there are a few species that crevice gardeners cherish. These offer fuzzy, silver buns embedded with showy, circular, upturned funnel-shaped flowers in summer. Grow them in deep, limy soils to accommodate their long taproots. Intolerant of winter wet, the following can be grown in crevice conditions. The plant known to gardeners as *C. suendermannii* (Z3), **bottom**, from SW Bulgaria and NE Greece boasts rich pink vases. *C. boissieri* (Z3), **top**, from Spain, has large shimmering white to pink flowers on silky silver mats reaching 30cm (12in) wide by 5cm (2in) high. *C. boissieri* ssp. *compactus* (Z7) has pure white to light pink flowers. Honorable mention: the Turkish *C. assyricus* (Z7) for its more distinct leaf rosettes.

CYCLAMEN
SOWBREAD

Family	Primulaceae
General habit	Tuberous perennials
Origin	Mostly the Mediterranean
Garden needs	Sun/part shade, dry

Cyclamen are excellent crevice plants, as many grow in such a habitat in nature. There is a cyclamen blooming for almost every month of the year, though their decorative foliage stands alone even without flowers. They are easy to grow from seed and naturalize in gardens. Most appreciate some summer dryness. *C. hederifolium* (Z5), **top**, blooms in fall with white to pink flowers over patterned, ivy-shaped leaves. *C. coum* (Z5) has round leaves and blooms in February. In April, *C. repandum* (Z7), **bottom**, bursts forth to sneak in a show just before summer. Rounding out the seasons, the summer-blooming *C. purpurascens* (Z3), **middle**, is both highly fragrant and the hardiest; it requires water during growth.

DAPHNE

Family	Thymelaeceae
General habit	Evergreen and deciduous shrubs
Origin	Eurasia
Garden needs	Sunny, regular water

The crevice-worthy varieties of *Daphne* are mostly evergreen, long-lived, and compact. They earn their place by smothering themselves in fragrant flowers from crystal white to deep pink, and many repeat bloom. Although soil-adaptable, they like well-drained alkaline conditions. Their growth can be slow at first but they are worth the wait. Daphnes detest transplanting and should be left in place. Some will root easily from cuttings, while others must be grafted on the roots of more robust species. Some are willing from seed, which has produced a range of amenable hybrids for rock gardens. The best daphne for the crevice garden is the prostrate *Daphne jasminea* Delphi form (Z7) at 2.5cm (1in) high. Unlike others, it is not terribly fragrant but has bicolor flowers, white above and deep crimson underneath. The hardier form (Z5b) is upright. *D. petraea* (Z6) is one of the most compact. *D. malyana* (Z7), **bottom**, from Montenegro, is semi-evergreen with pure white flowers, 15cm (6in) tall. *D. oleoides* (Z7) and *D. domini* (Z3), **middle**, are bigger species with orange or red berries. Slow-growing *D. velenovskyi* (Z3), **top**, boasts light pink flowers on a compact plant.

DELOSPERMA

HARDY ICE PLANT

Family	Aizoaceae
General habit	Succulent mats and buns
Origin	High mountains of South and East Africa
Garden needs	Sun, regular water, dry winters

Buns or ground-hugging, spreading carpets, delospermas have daisy-like flowers that shimmer like melting ice and require the sun to open. Bloom periods range from long to extra long. Cold-tolerant in gardens with winter drainage and summer water, they also respond to rich soil. *D. congestum* (Z4), **middle**, perhaps the hardiest, is a flat bun of rubbery leaves and stemless yellow flowers with white centers. *D. sphalmanthoides* (Z5), **bottom**, is the less-xeric and true alpine baby at 2.5 x 10cm (1 x 4in) with magenta flowers that obscure its blue-green leaves. The larger *D. nubigenum* (Z5, or 4) is a fast-spreading bathmat of leaves like pudgy toes with gold flowers. With red winter foliage it's an ideal skirt for the rock garden. *D. cooperi* (Z5) is perhaps most climate-adaptable, aggressive, and large. Try *D. sutherlandii* (Z6), **top**, for yellow-eyed, pink flowers. All are easy from seed or cuttings and happy to hybridize to supply a reblooming rainbow of all colors but true blue.

DIANTHUS
ROCK PINK

Family	Caryophyllaceae
General habit	Mats and buns
Origin	Eurasia
Garden needs	Sunny, regular water

Evergreen, mid-season blooming and sometimes fragrant, this genus provides a huge range of species and cultivars. They are great beginner plants as they're easy to grow from seed and cuttings, maturing quickly to bloom in neutral to alkaline soil. Favorites include *D. erinaceus*, now known as *D. webbianus* (Z3), with tight domes with starry light pink flowers just above; *D. microlepis* (Z3) is a classic species rarely exceeding 10cm (4in) across, the variety *deginii* is pictured **bottom**. Honorable mentions to D. *freynii* (Z3), *D. arpadianus* var. *pumilus* (Z6), **top**, and D. *myrtinervius* var. *caespitosus* (Z3) as some of the smallest and tightest of the genus which feature a range of flower colors from light to dark pink.

DIONYSIA

Family	Primulaceae
General habit	Congested buns
Origin	Iran to Central Asia
Garden needs	Bright shade/moist soil, dry tops

Named after the Greek party-god, these hairy-leaved buns bloom in a range of colours. They are often found in nature growing vertically, facing north, and even upside-down on limestone overhangs, usually protected from hot sun and rain overhead. The ones listed here achieve heights of 7.5cm (3in). The easiest species, *D. aretioides* (Z6), is a globe of green felt with tiny fruity-fragrant trumpets; grown from cuttings, the cultivar 'Gravetye' is pictured **top**. The second easiest, *D. involucrata* (Z6), has veined crystalline leaves and reddish stems to hold up bright-eyed hot pink flowers. Highly variable and slow-growing *Dionysia tapetodes* (Z6), **bottom**, forms dense cushions with tightly packed rosettes. Always considered a challenge, they are usually cultivated in tufa or in an alpine house, but gardeners in dryer climates can grow at least these two in shady crevices outdoors, usually steep and north-facing in sand, but with deeper access to heavier, nutritious soil. A bright but not sunny spot with excellent air circulation is critical.

DRABA
WHITLOW GRASS

Family	Brassicaceae
General habit	Miniature evergreen buns
Origin	Europe, Asia, North America
Garden needs	Sun, dry

The drabas are a large genus with early white or yellow flowers. Our favorites form tight buns of congested rosettes on plants only 5–8cm (2–3in) high. Some are easily grown, gently self-sowing into quaint little colonies. Excess water is not to their liking. Our choices are approximately the same size, 5–8cm (2–3in) tall and wide, blooming yellow. *D. rigida* (Z3) from eastern Turkey and Armenia has rigid, hairy-margined, dark green leaves and upward-facing flowers on tiny thready stems. *D. rigida* var. *bryoides* (Z4), **top**, looks like moss, as the name suggests, with protruding yellow racemes. *D. polytricha* (Z5), **bottom**, means 'excessively hairy'. *D. acaulis* (Z3) makes a furry little bun with stemless flowers that sit right on the foliage. *D. aizoides* (Z4) is larger, very easy, and the most climate-adaptable.

DRACOCEPHALUM
DRAGON'S HEAD

Family	Lamiaceae
General habit	Mat-forming forbs
Origin	Temperate Northern Hemisphere
Garden needs	Full sun, dry

These pest-resistant herbs carry racemes of unique blue, pink, or white hooded flowers in summer for a good duration. They are quick and easy from seed, a perfect choice for the beginning home-grower. All seem to like a dry top and tolerate drought. Among the small rock-huggers are *D. botryoides* (Z3), **left**, a 10 x 25cm (4 x 10in) cushion of lightly fuzzy, lacey gray-green leaves and pink blooms. A classic, *D. paulsenii* (Z4), from the Tien Shan, is a low thyme-like mat with big warm blue flowers resembling tiny catnip.

DRYAS
MOUNTAIN AVENS

Family	Rosaceae
General habit	Mat-forming shrubs
Origin	Circumpolar Arctic-alpine
Garden needs	Sun, regular water

The dryas are unique for the rose family in that they feature eight petals (sometimes more), rather than the usual five. Their evergreen scalloped foliage, reminiscent of tiny oak leaves, sits above flat mats of woody, ground-hugging branches which can reach widths of 1m (3ft) or more. Above the mats are cheery white or yellow flowers followed by fluffy ornamental seedheads. Dryas are found in nature growing on a wide range of substrates and are consequently not picky in garden situations, though they fare best in cool, limy soils in full sun. *D. octopetala* (Z2), **top**, in flower and, **bottom**, in seed, is the most common, wide-ranging, and showy species both in nature and in gardens, bearing white flowers with yellow centers. *D. drummondii* (Z3) carries fascinating, drooping yellow flowers. *D.* x *suendermannii* (Z3) is a hybrid between the two.

ECHINOCEREUS
HEDGEHOG CACTUS

Family	Cactaceae
General habit	Cushions and clumps
Origin	Southwestern USA and Mexico
Garden needs	Full sun, dry

An ideal group of cacti for rock gardens because of their compact form, winter hardiness, and variety of flower color, *Echinocereus* are often native to crevices. All species are relatively slow from seed and cuttings rot easily, needing winter dryness to be hardy. *E. coccineus* (Z4) is the hardiest species, *E. triglochidiatus* f. *inermis* (Z5), **top**, is spineless with chubby green bodies below red, goblet-shaped flowers. *E. dasyacanthus* (Z6), **bottom**, are variable short-spined plants topped with massive water lily-like flowers in a range of tropical colors. *E. viridiflorus* (Z5) has humble fragrant flowers, and usually red and white spination. It is often the most moisture-tolerant species, used as a rootstock for grafting other tricky species.

EDRAIANTHUS
ROCKBELL

Family	Campanulaceae
General habit	Dwarf forbs
Origin	European mountains
Garden needs	Sun, regular water, lime

These are indispensable plants featuring striking upturned blue or white, solitary or clustered flowers in late spring and early summer. Like all Campanulaceae, they are easy and quick from seed. *E. pumilio* (Z3), **bottom**, is the smallest and most beautiful of those mentioned here, with spiky, congested rosettes supporting glimmering light-blue upturned bells only 2.5cm (1in) high. Its dwarfest forms are often fictionally labelled *E. owerinianus,* in reference to the super-rare *Muehlbergella oweriana*. *E. serpyllifolius* (Z3), **top**, is a little bigger and looser. *E. niveus* (Z3) has white flowers in clusters on dark green cushions.

ERIGERON
FLEABANE

Family	Asteraceae
General habit	Dwarf forbs
Origin	Worldwide
Garden needs	Sun, regular water

Easy from seed or division, fleabane is an indispensable crevice garden genus. *E. compositus* (Z2) is a variable North American Arctic-alpine species, boasting white or blue-tinted flowers above the hairy, gray-green basal foliage. It is reliable and self-sowing. *E. tener* (Z4) is native to crevices and ledge habitats in the American Great Basin, bearing blue daisies on a clean, hamburger-bun shaped plant. *E. chrysopsidis* (Z4) hosts bright yellow daisies rising just 10cm (4in) above a clump of skinny gray foliage, its cultivar 'Grand Ridge', **top**. The classic *E. scopulinus* (Z5), **bottom**, is a tiny little daisy that forms an easily divided puddle of dark, evergreen leaves, with flowers not more than 2.5cm (1in) tall. Kenton's favorite is *E. compactus* (Z4), a fine little plant with big white flowers for desert gardens.

ERINUS ALPINUS
ALPINE BALSAM

Family	Plantaginaceae
General habit	Dwarf herbs
Origin	European mountains
	Dwarf, short-lived, rosette-forming evergreen
Garden needs	Sun/part shade, regular water

This is a cheery little alpine (Z4) that will happily self-sow and form delightful colonies topped with masses of purple or white, 10cm (4in) tall, fragrant flowers. While it reseeds enough for some gardeners to call it a weed and does not require a crevice at all, it is a useful filler plant for larger gardens below cliffs and the areas immediately around a crevice garden to hold out against actual weeds. Its miniature rosettes are easily scratched out when a spot for a finer plant is needed.

ERIOGONUM
WILD BUCKWHEAT

Family	Polygonaceae
General habit	Evergreen mats and buns and shrubs
Origin	Western North America
Garden needs	Full sun, dry

For the driest, hottest, and most sun-baked parts of the crevice garden, *Eriogonum* is a large and captivating genus with white, yellow, pink, or red pom-pom flowers. Easily grown from seed, its biggest enemy is overwatering. *E. umbellatum* has many forms, the best being Utah's *E. umbellatum* var. *porteri* (Z3), **bottom**, which has yellow flowers fading to red above a tight mat of green leaves that also turn red in winter. It reaches 10 x 15cm (4 x 6in). *E. ovalifolium* var. *nivale* (Z3), **top**, is the most climate-adaptable subspecies of this showy species, forming a silver mat with usually cream flowers on thin stems. *E. thymoides* (Z3) is unsurprisingly a tiny thyme-like bush with miniature creamy-white pom-pom flowers. The choicest species is *E. kennedyi* (Z3) at 2.5 (1in) tall, resembling silver moss.

ERITRICHIUM
ALPINE FORGET-ME-NOT

Family	Boraginaceae
General habit	Compact cushions
Origin	Circumpolar Arctic-alpine
Garden needs	Bright shade, regular water in summer, dryish in winter, tufa

Anyone who has succeeded in growing this plant has demonstrated an understanding of its exacting requirements and origins. As with many high alpines, winter wet is the enemy, so think of drainage and the pH of a tufa crevice. The 'King of the Alps', *E. nanum* (Z4), **left**, is a circumpolar Arctic-alpine cushion from mountaintops. Gardeners in dryer climates have had easier luck with *E. howardii* (Z3) of Montana and Wyoming.

ESCOBARIA
FOXTAIL OR PINCUSHION CACTI

Family	Cactaceae
General habit	Mounds and buns
Origin	North America
Garden needs	Full sun, dry

Cutting-edge crevice gardeners covet the superior cold-hardiness and relative moisture-tolerance of these single stems or clustered mounds. Star-shaped blooms range from earth tones to hot pinks. Honey-flowered *E. missouriensis* is native from grassland to desert crevice, adapting widely to gardens. Its usually flat but sometimes 10cm (4in) body is studded with red fruits. The precocious, reblooming *E. vivipara* (Z3) is even more adaptable of which var. *bisbeeana* is pictured, **top**. Its hot pink blooms precede sweet, snackable fruits. *E. sneedii* (Z4) 10 x 25cm (4 x 10in) is a dome of felted buttons with a variety of flower colors. It comes from rock heaps in the wild and masters them in gardens. *E. sneedii* and its kin take easily from cuttings planted directly into the hottest, driest cracks but also tolerate wetter and even humid climates. *E. sneedii* ssp. *leei* (Z4), **bottom**, is the choicest – smaller, with politely inward-pointing spines.

Ferns

Above: *Polypodium amorphum*
Right top: *Adiantum aleuticum* var.
subpumilum
Right middle: *Asplenium trichomanes*
Right bottom: *Asplenium ceterach*

The dwarf ferns are in a class unto themselves.
Reproduced by spores rather than seeds and often
tolerant of deep shade and summer drought, the
four presented here are all less than 15cm (6in) tall
and are often crevice-dwellers in nature. Lime-loving
Asplenium ceterach (Z7) is a European 'resurrection'
fern that can spring back from desiccation after
getting wet. *Asplenium trichomanes* (Z5), a classic
circumboreal fern, is commonly found growing in
ruins and rock walls. *Myriopteris gracillima* (Z5), the
lace lip fern, is the smallest in its kin. Moisture-loving
ferns include *Polypodium amorphum* (Z6), a North
American evergreen alpine from igneous rock cracks,
and the most diminutive maidenhair fern: *Adiantum
aleuticum* var. *subpumilum* (Z4) from Vancouver Island,
only 13cm (5in).

GENTIANA
GENTIAN

Family	Gentianaceae
General habit	Mats and clumps
Origin	Circumpolar
Garden needs	Sun, regular water

Unlike many rock garden plants, gentians are heavy feeders that thrive in humus and clay-based loam. Most prefer full or bright sun, but not too much heat. All are easy, if slow, from seed, and the division of old plants is a simple matter. We recommend the super classic *G. acaulis* (Z3) group, **bottom**, which all shout with the largest blue trumpets of any of the dwarf gentians. They grow as a stoloniferous mat of glossy, evergreen leaves and reach a height of 10cm (4in). *G. verna* (Z3), **top**, is shorter at 7.5cm (3in) with star-shaped flowers in the rich blues one expects from any good gentian. Finally, the easier, and drier-adapting *G. septemfida* (Z3) and its kin are taller, at 15–40cm (6–15in), bloom in late summer, are herbaceous and form taproots.

GLOBULARIA
GLOBE DAISY

Family	Plantaginaceae
General habit	Clump and mat-forming subshrubs
Origin	European mountains and beyond
Garden needs	Sunny, regular water

These are the perfect plants that no crevice gardener should be without. Most form dark evergreen mats of glossy green leaves, out of which poke the cutest little blue or white pom-poms on tiny stems. All are easy to grow in full sun and well-drained calcareous soil, and are super-easy to propagate from cuttings. The mainstay *G. cordifolia* (Z3) forms flat mats 45cm (18in) or more across. The smallest, usually labelled *G. repens* 'Alba' (Z4b), **bottom**, is an even more diminutive plant that conforms to the very rocks over which it creeps, with flowers held tight against the foliage. Both have white varieties. *G. incanescens* (Z4), **top**, forms an 8 x 12cm (3 x 5in) congested clump of rounded leaves below characteristic steel-blue flowers.

GYPSOPHILA
BABY'S BREATH

Family	Caryophyllaceae
General habit	Tight buns and mats
Origin	Europe to Middle East
Garden needs	Sun, regular water, lime

The name of this genus comes from a Greek word meaning lime-loving, a definite clue to their cultivation. *G. cerastioides* [new name *Acanthophyllum cerastioides*] (Z3), or alpine baby's breath, forms loose tufts of soft leaves below white flowers with pink veins. *G. repens* 'Rosea' (Z3), **top**, a long-lived and divisible classic, features pink flowers. *G. aretioides* (Z4), **bottom**, is the best and most difficult – a hard bun from the Middle East that grows to only 10 x 20cm (4 x 8in) with surface-embedded flowers.

HABERLEA
RESURRECTION PLANT

Family	Gesneriaceae
General habit	Stemless rosette-forming evergreens
Origin	Limestone cliffs in Greece and Bulgaria
Garden needs	Shade, moist/dry, lime

These hardy African violet relatives are for the well-drained shady nook of the crevice garden, flowering blue with an orange-speckled throat. A 'resurrection plant', *Haberlea* species can dry out in the summer, appear dead, then revive with the first watering. Older plants can be divided. *H. rhodopensis* (Z5), **bottom**, is the most commonly grown of this spare genus. The plant known to gardeners as *H. ferdinandi-coburgii* (Z5) is sometimes thought to be a form of the above with larger leaves and flowers. The gem of them is the pure white, class-act *H. rhodopensis* 'Virginalis' (Z5), **top**. All are 15 x 15cm (6 x 6in).

HELICHRYSUM
EVERLASTING

Family	Asteraceae
General habit	Evergreen mat-forming herbs
Origin	Drakensberg Mountains and Eurasia
Garden needs	Sun, regular water

Like an exotic cousin of *Antennaria* (pussytoes), these rosette-forming mats challenge gardeners by demanding moisture but sharp drainage and protection from winter wetness. Some have flowers that open and close with daylight. They are easily propagated by cuttings. *H. sessilioides* (Z5), **top**, features silver-haired leaves no higher than 1cm (1/2in) with white flowers sitting right on the foliage. *H. milfordiae* (Z5), **bottom**, is without question the most beautiful, a compact cushion of soft, fuzzy rosettes below the large, papery, everlasting white flowers, with undersides of a deep red. Finally, *H. praecurrens* (Z6) is just 2cm (3/4in) tall

HETEROTHECA
GOLDENASTER

Family	Asteraceae
General habit	Evergreen mat
Origin	American West
Garden needs	Full sun, dry

This genus of miniature yellow sunflowers is dominated by unruly bedheads, but *H. jonesii* (Z3) is unique. From rock crevices in Utah, it forms a tight gray rock-caressing mat, 1 x 30cm (1/2 x 12in), with spontaneous stemless yellow sunflowers. It grows well from cuttings and can self-sow, and unsurprisingly requires sun and dryness. An introduction called 'Goldhill' (*H. jonesii* x *H. villosa*) (Z3) is a round 10cm (4in) dome of foliage and larger flowers. Larger at 20 x 30cm (8 x 12in) but worthwhile, *H. pumila* (Z4), **left**, is from alpine and subalpine areas in the Rockies.

HORMATHOPHYLLA
(FORMERLY PTILOTRICHUM)
SPINY MADWORT

Family	Brassicaceae
General habit	Dwarf shrubs
Origin	Mediterranean Europe and temperate Asia
Garden needs	Full sun, dry

These high-mountain crucifers resemble shrubby little wallflowers. Grow them in dry and sunny conditions and you will be rewarded with mounded domes of twisted and densely branched yet delicate shrubs. They are very easy to grow from seed and are long-lived self-sowers in the limy garden. *H. spinosa* (Z3), **bottom**, growing to 15 x 45cm (6 x 18in), comes from the limestone of the Spanish Sierra Nevada. High spring finds it covered in with white alyssum-like flowers. Even finer, but requiring more space at 30 x 60cm (12 x 24 in), is *H. spinosa* 'Roseum' (Z3), **top**, with rose-pink flowers.

IRIS
IRIS

Family	Iridaceae
General habit	Evergreen, bulbous and herbaceous perennials
Origin	Circumpolar
Garden needs	Full sun, dry/moist

This is a diverse genus with diverse needs, some species strongly benefiting from the crevice. The easiest are the miniature bearded *I. attica* (Z5), *I. pumila* (Z3), *I. reichenbachii* (Z5), and *I. suaveolens* (Z4). Their flat leaves lend variety among the buns and cushions. Another section, the challenging Oncocyclus, is the perfect crevice garden iris with small stature, huge flowers, and deep roots. *I. cristata* (Z3), **top**, makes pleasing clumps and its rhizomes creep right over the rocks. The easiest to acquire and grow is the velvet purple-black *I. paradoxa* (Z5). Like many, *I. grossheimii* (Z6) and *I. sprengeri* (Z6), **bottom**, are pale with dark veins. Plant their moisture-intolerant rhizomes barely covered by gravel, letting their roots reach below into fertile soil. They are easily divided but not too often, preserving their deep roots. The bulbous *I. reticulata* group (Z5) is also a good choice where the soil is nutritious. Seeds are often tedious to germinate, usually requiring both careful scarification and stratification.

JUNELLIA

Family	Verbenaceae
General habit	Mat-forming shrubs
Origin	South America
Garden needs	Full sun, dry

These woody, often evergreen shrubs are adapted to mountain, windy, dry, and maritime conditions. Those that cower flat on the ground under Patagonia's relentless wind fit nicely in crevice gardens. The completely flat and sweetly fragrant *J. micrantha* (Z3), **left**, is most cultivated by rock gardeners, looking like a miniature thyme yet blooming at its growth tips with two-toned lavender and white flower clusters. Another one to try is *J. congesta* (Z3).

KALMIOPSIS LEACHIANA

Family	Ericaceae
General habit	Evergreen shrublet
Origin	Siskiyou Mountains
Garden needs	Sun, moist acidic soil

K. leachiana (Z7), **left**, is a dwarf ericaceous shrub of the highest order, whose native range is restricted to the Siskiyou Mountains of southern Oregon. It is the only species in the genus and, as its name implies, resembles a *Kalmia*. Only 20cm (8in) tall, it features dark green leaves and bright-pink bell flowers on a dome-shaped plant. Although tolerant of full sun, it should be given the same treatment as dwarf rhododendrons with consistently moist, well-drained, humus-rich, acid soils. The one commonly found in cultivation is called 'Umpqua Form'.

LEONTOPODIUM
EDELWEISS

Family	Asteraceae
General habit	Dwarf forb
Origin	Eurasian mountains
Garden needs	Sunny, regular water

Edelweiss is a classic rock garden plant perfectly suited for crevice gardens. *Leontopodium* means 'lion's paws', describing the fuzzy bracts that make up the flower. For mountainous European countries, it is a national symbol of their rugged alpine beauty. Although easily grown, the species are typically short-lived perennials and as true alpines they prefer sunny but cool conditions in the garden. Start with *L. nivale ssp. alpinum*, *L. nivale*, **left**, and *L. nanum*, both are Z3 and 5cm (2in) tall.

LEWISIA
BITTERROOT

Family	Montiaceae
General habit	Succulent evergreen rosette or forb
Origin	Western North America
Garden needs	Full sun, moist in spring, dry in winter

All lewisias are middle- to high-elevation succulent plants that experience snow cover and most can be classed as true alpines, producing showy, long-lasting blooms. The two broad groups are evergreen and deciduous, with the latter being ephemeral, dormant in summer and reappearing with winter rains. The evergreen species produce succulent rosettes, grow easily in dry climates and absolutely require crevices in wetter ones. All lewisias are easily propagated by seed or cuttings. The largest, at 30 x 30cm (12 x 12in) or more, is *L. cotyledon* (Z5) and its colorful hybrids. It is the most widespread in cultivation, with tongue-shaped leaves and multiple rosettes. The diminutive *L. columbiania* 'Rosea' (Z3) has shimmering rosy-red flowers and tightly packed leaves. The most famous of the deciduous species (named for Meriwether Lewis) is *L. rediviva* (Z3), **top**, which boasts grand pale pink to white flowers on petite plants 5cm (2in) tall. *L. nevadensis* 'Rosea', **middle**, and *L. brachycalyx* (Z6) are also tiny deciduous crevice specimens. We cannot talk about *Lewisia* without mentioning the closely related evergreen *Lewisiopsis tweedyi* (Z5), **bottom**, known as the 'Queen of the Rock Garden'. Grow it like *Lewisia cotyledon* and you'll discover why!

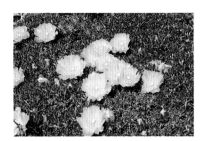

MAIHUENIA

Family	Cactaceae
General habit	Low mats
Origin	Highlands of Argentina and Chile
Garden needs	Full sun, dry

The cold-hardy 'missing link' between cacti and 'normal' plants, *Maihuenia* deals with high winds and burial by grit, producing large, tulip-like flowers in early summer. *M. poeppigii* (Z5), **left**, is a bright green mat with pale yellow-white flowers, growing slowly up to 1m (3ft) across in gardens. It tolerates summer irrigation and a little winter wetness, and is easy in dry continental gardens. *M. patagonica* (Z6a) is a slower-growing darker-green dome maybe 20cm (8in) wide, with pinkish-tan suffused flowers, rare and more difficult to cultivate. Both species can be grown from cuttings and require scarification or stratification to germinate.

MOLTKIA PETRAEA

Family	Boraginaceae
General habit	Dwarf shrub
Origin	Southern Europe, Asia
Garden needs	Full sun, dry

Moltkia are blue, white, or yellow sun-bathing shrubs and forbs with tubular flowers. The Balkan *M. petrea* (Z5), **left**, is the heart-throb of gardeners, crowned in high summer by masses of true-blue pendent blooms on a blue-gray 45 x 60cm (1½ x 2ft) plant with an appearance and pruning needs not unlike lavender. Grown from cuttings and seeds, this provides the kind of summer blues you will want in your life.

OXALIS

WOOD SORREL

Family	Oxalidaceae
General habit	Tuberous forbs
Origin	Worldwide
Garden needs	Sun, dry in summer, not hot

This is a well-behaved branch of a big family and a desirable group for crevice gardens, tolerant of low temperatures and summer drought. Tubers go dormant in summer and come back to life in the spring and fall. Most only reach 7.5cm (3in) tall. *O. adenophylla* (Z5), **top**, from high elevation talus in Chile and Argentina, is the most commonly grown species, with white to pink flowers with dark purple centers opening from twisting buds held above silver-blue clover-like foliage. *O. melanosticta* (Z8) from South Africa forms clumps of fuzzy gray spoon-shaped leaves appearing with fall rains, followed by unexpectedly large yellow flowers. *O. erythrorhiza* (Z4) is the gem of the genus, an alpine bun-former with yellow shamrock flowers held right against the foliage. Try also *O. enneaphylla* (Z6) and *O. adenophylla* x *laciniata* (Z5), **bottom**.

PAEDEROTA BONAROTA

Family	Plantaginaceae
General habit	Julian Alps
Origin	Clump-forming forb
Garden needs	Sunny, regular water

An uncommon endemic, *Paederota bonarota* (Z6), **left**, favors high-elevation, alpine limestone crevices. Although variable in size, the best forms reach only 5cm (2in) high with hairy, toothed herbaceous foliage below racemes of purple-indigo blue flowers. Grow in dryer conditions in well-drained neutral soil in full sun. It is not commonly seen in rock gardens, but is a pretty cool plant.

PENSTEMON
BEARD-TONGUE

Family	Plantaginaceae
General habit	Creeping, dwarf shrubs
Origin	Mostly western North America
Garden needs	Full sun, dry

A New World genus, and a contingent well suited to the dry crevice garden. *P. davidsonii* (Z3) is an evergreen mat of the far western alpine with crenulate, glossy-green leaves and purple flowers. The related *P. rupicola* (Z3), **top**, boasts scarlet-red flowers over glaucous foliage. Both take well from cuttings and stay under 7.5cm (3in) in height. Smaller and more challenging is the dryland *P. yampaensis* (Z4), a bun-like tuft of linear leaves with classic penstemon sky-blue throaty flowers. *P. caespitosus* (Z3), **bottom**, and its many kin spread by prostrate, creeping stems to form sizable mats. The most fickle and pretty of them is *P.* var. *desertipicti* (Z4), more compact with red-violet flowers and silver-gray foliage. Don't forget *P. arenicola* (Z4) and crevice-native *P. petiolatus* (Z4).

PETROPHYTUM
ROCK SPIRAEA

Family	Rosaceae
General habit	Bun- or mat-forming shrubs
Origin	Western North America
Garden needs	Full sun, dry

You know you're on the right path when a Latin binomial translates directly to 'rock plant'. Spiraea-like blooms of creamy-white flowers stand above invisibly gnarled ancient mats that inhabit American cliffs and crevices to reach 45cm (18in) across. The most common species, *P. caespitosum* (Z3), **bottom**, forms mats of blue-green leaves with bright autumn colors and upright flower spikes or even panicles on stems of variable height. *P. hendersonii* (Z5), **top**, differs in habit, tending to form a small green bush of loose rosettes, and rising higher to 10cm (4in). A true alpine, it follows cracks and crevices on some of the Olympic Mountains' loftiest summits. The rare *P. cinerascens* (Z5) is just as easy from seed or cuttings.

PETUNIA (SYN. NIEREMBERGIA)

Family	Solanaceae
General habit	Evergreen shrub
Origin	Dry steppes of South America
Garden needs	Full sun, dry

Petunia patagonica (Z5b), **left**, from the steppe of South America that has long lured alpine gardeners, is a slow-growing evergreen mounding shrub bearing curious white to yellow solanaceous flowers with purple veining just 1cm (½in) wide. Happy plants in a good, dry climate can sprawl more than 30cm (12in) wide but remain only 15cm (6in) high. A collector's plant, it is often shy to flower in cultivation and should be given full sun with perfect drainage.

PHLOX

MOSS PHLOX

Family	Polemoniaceae
General habit	Bun- and carpet-forming sub-shrubs
Origin	North America
Garden needs	Full sun, dry/moist, well drained

From North American prairie, open woodland, and alpine habitats hail the 'microphloxes', which find favor in the crevice garden. Most available today are a melange of species and hybrids including *P. kelseyi*, *P. bifida*, *P. subulata*, *P. nivalis*, *P. hoodii*, and P. *douglasii*. Some of the rock garden phloxes such as the eastern *P. subulata* hybrids are too large for smaller crevice gardens, but their splashes of intense spring color (phlox means flame) can be used around rock bases and in low areas. Tried and true are the western *P. douglasii* x *subulata* hybrids such as 'Crackerjack' (Z3), **bottom**, 'Boranovice' (Z3), **top**, and 'Zigeunerblut' (Z3), which form tight, 2.5–12cm (1–5in) mounds of needle-like leaves that are hidden during flowering. There are many more, and every single one is as charming as a plant can be.

PHYSOPLEXIS COMOSA

DEVIL'S CLAW

Family	Campanulaceae
General habit	Clump-forming forb
Origin	European Alps
Garden needs	Sun, regular water, lime

Physoplexis comosa (Z5), **left**, a 'one of a kind' species from the Italian and Austrian Alps, captivates all who cross its path. Farrer referred to it as 'the strangest of all the children on the cliff'. Formerly called *Phytuma comosum*, this unique individual, the only species of the genus, features glossy toothed leaves and umbels of lavender flowers darkening at the petal tips, which fuse to form a spike. It reaches a height and width of 6 x 8cm (2 x 3in). It is not the easiest plant in cultivation, and as a limestone-loving plant, it definitely benefits by being grown in a tufa crevice with even moisture.

207

PLANT PROFILES

POLYGALA
MILKWORT

Family	Polygalaceae
General habit	Mats or forbs
Origin	Europe
Garden needs	Sun, regular water, lime

The globally distributed *Polygala* is a huge genus that in ancient times was thought to increase milk yields in cattle. Of the many known species, *P. chamaebuxus* (Z5), **top**, and *P. calcarea* (Z5) are rock garden classics. The former is an eye-catching bicolored clown, while the latter forms a prostrate mat with 5cm (2in) racemes of funky-shaped clear blue flowers. Both resent drying out and are difficult in hot climates. *P. calcarea* 'Lillet' is pictured **bottom**.

POTENTILLA NITIDA
CINQUEFOIL

Family	Rosaceae
General habit	Perennial mat
Origin	Italian Alps and Apennines
Garden needs	Sun, regular water, lime

Potentilla nitida (Z3), **left**, is a choicest-of-choice gem. This minute, silver-green, trifoliate jewel fairly shines in the sun, with single rose-like flowers. It almost looks like a fancy, miniature, evergreen strawberry. Its tidy mats reach 2.5cm (1in) high with flowers atop the foliage. As it comes from cooler alpine regions, don't let it dry out and give it shade from the hottest sun. It is adaptable to many climates and worthy of any collection.

PRIMULA
PRIMROSE

Family	Primulaceae
General habit	Perennials
Origin	Global distribution
Garden needs	Sun or shade, regular water

A genus in a wide-ranging family full of familiar rock garden plants, this one offers numerous choices from the taller monsoonal and moist-meadow species of central Asia to the rock-hugging species of the Alps. Dwarf for the crevice garden, *P. marginata* (Z3), **bottom**, is a classic of the French Alpes-Maritimes with leaf margins gilded with farina to frame various shades of light blue flowers. *P x pubescens* (Z4) lacks this edging, but offers near-succulent leaves under a multitude of flower colors. Another classic, *P. allionii* (Z4), **top**, is from limestone cliffs and crevices in the French and Italian Alps.

PTEROCEPHALUS
PINCUSHION FLOWER

Family	Dipsacaceae
General habit	Low, creeping mats
	Mediterranean Europe to
Origin	Central Asia
Garden needs	Sun, dry

At least three species are grown in sunny and dry crevice gardens, hailing from dry European mountain regions. These long-lived creepers can layer themselves as they spread up to 1.2m (4 ft) over rocks and spill over edges, but never rise more than 5cm (2in). Long-blooming in summer, the pink pincushion flowers are embedded in the foliage and are followed by feathery seedheads. *P. depressus* (Z5) from Morocco has the finest dissected leaves of the three named here, with dusky-pink flowers and greener leaves than the usual gray-green. Similar is *P. pinardii* (Z4), **top**, from Turkey, and *P. perennis* (Z6), pictured **bottom** in seed, with more rounded, glaucous-green leaves. They are very easy to grow from cuttings.

RAMONDA
PYRENEAN VIOLET

Family	Gesneriaceae
General habit	Stemless, rosette-forming
	evergreens
Origin	Mediterranean mountains
Garden needs	Shade, wet/dry

This is a genus that demands a cooler north-facing situation and a limy, humusy vertical crevice or tufa, moist during growth. From the center of each rosette rises a 10cm (4in) stem bearing blue or white flowers in spring. Ramondas are 'resurrection plants' that can revive after almost complete desiccation. All three species are similar in appearance with dense rosettes of ground-hugging, hairy, crenate leaves. The multiple rosettes are easily divided. The seed is like dust and the tiny seedlings must never dry out. *R. myconi* (Z5) is from the Pyrenees of northeast Spain, *R. nathaliae* (Z6) is from Serbia and Macedonia, and *R. serbica* (Z6) comes from the Balkan peninsula. Pictured **top** is *R. myconi* 'Grandiflora' and **bottom** *R. nathaliae* 'Alba'.

RAOULIA
SCABWORT

Family	Asteraceae
General habit	Tight carpets or buns
Origin	New Zealand
Garden needs	Sun, regular water/dry

R. eximia has famously been called the 'vegetable sheep' as it billows up looking like a sheep on a steep hillside at distance. *R. australis* (Z4), **left**, is probably the most common species in cultivation, with perfectly flat mats of gray foliage studded with minute yellow 'sunflowers' in summer. Honorable mentions to *R. haastii* (Z7), *R. hookeri* (Z6), and R. *mammillaris* (Z6). Although virtually flat, all should be planted with potential spread in mind as they can grow 1m (3ft) wide.

RHODODENDRON

Family	Ericaceae
General habit	Dwarf, evergreen shrubs
Origin	Global distribution
Garden needs	Sun, moist acidic soil

You might be forgiven if rhododenrons don't jump to mind for the crevice garden, but you can get your rhodie fix with high-elevation dwarfs for well-drained, acidic soil that never dries. They want sun for bud set and tight growth, but they also want to remain cool. *R. campylogynum* Myrtilloides Group (Z5), **bottom**, is variable, but the smallest varieties form dense globes reaching 30 x 30cm (12 x 12in) with glossy 1cm (1/2in) leaves, perfectly proportioned to its nodding purple bell-shaped flowers. *R. calostrotum* ssp. *keleticum* (Z5), **top**, has tiny, glossy, lanceolate leaves and upright, deep lilac-pink flowers on a variable-sized but dwarf plant.

SAPONARIA

SOAPWORT

Family	Caryophyllaceae
General habit	Hummock-forming perennials, mats, buns
Origin	Eurasia
Garden needs	Sun, regular water

Saponaria gives beautiful splashes of bright pink or white in early to midsummer. All in the genus are sun-lovers and must be given a bright but not baking spot with neutral to limy soil; they are surprisingly tolerant of drought. *S.* x *olivana* (Z7) forms tight mats of glossy green leaves supporting virtually stemless and large medium-pink flowers, 5 x 25cm (2 x 10in). *S. ocymoides* 'Rubra Compacta' (Z5) is a diminutive form of the classic, *S. ocymoides* (Z3), covered in rich pink flowers. *S.* 'Bressingham' (Z5), **top**, is also a classic beginner's rock garden hybrid. Lastly, the appropriately named *S. pumilio* (Z5), **bottom**, is one of the smallest in both leaf and flower, and one of the tightest hummock formers with narrow leaves and pink upward-pointed trumpets. Most are easy to grow from seed or cuttings.

SAXIFRAGA
ROCKFOIL

Family	Saxifragaceae
General habit	Buns and carpets
Origin	Northern Hemisphere, Arctic and alpine
Garden needs	Sun, cool, regular water

Although the name translates literally as 'rock breaker', the 'rocks' in mind are gallstones as *Saxifraga* was once believed to cure them. Very much at home among rocks, these saxatile plants detest drought and heat and grow best in a cool and bright north-facing vertical crevice. Small bun- or mat-forming species reaching 5–10cm (2–4in), they can generally be divided into two groups: silver saxifrages and porophyllum saxifrages. The former typically have white flowers rising in panicles in early summer, while the latter start flowering as early as January and continue through April with a wide array of flower colors including white, yellow, red, pink, and even orange. The silver saxifrages root as they travel, so are easily propagated by division, and all grow easily from cuttings. For the silvers, try the single large rosetted and monocarpic *S. longifolia* (Z4), **top**, or the tiny *S. cochlearis* 'Minor' (Z3). Porophyllums include *S.* x *apiculata* (Z5), perfect for the beginner. For classier plants, try *S. burseriana* (Z4) and *S. marginata* (Z4). Some mossy saxifrages, a third group, may also be mentioned here as runners up: *S. cebennensis* (Z4) and *S. pubescens* (Z4), **bottom**. Finally, we can't leave out the beautiful circumpolar Arctic–alpine *S. oppositifolia* (Z2), **middle**.

SEMPERVIVUM
HOUSELEEK

Family	Crassulaceae
General habit	Rosetted succulents
Origin	Europe to the Near East mountains
Garden needs	Full sun/part shade, dry

The name means 'always living'. The quintessential versatile succulents, most increase rapidly and survive most situations; their offsets can be removed from the mother plant and simply pushed into crevices where they can regrow their fine, shallow roots. *S. arachnoideum* (Z3), **bottom**, the cobweb sempervivum and its hybrids, is one of the smaller ones with webbing strung from the points of the geometric leaves. The highly variable and commonly cultivated *S. tectorum* (Z2) has 2.5cm (1in) pointed leaves with often ruddy tips, a classic plant grown on roofs as it was believed to guard against lightning strikes. Diverse, colorful hybrids between these two and other species dominate nurseries, like the darling 'Jade' **top**. *S. heuffelii,* formerly *Jovibarba heuffelii,* (Z3) is a diverse and more contained choice for the collector.

SILENE
CAMPION, CATCHFLY

Family	Caryophyllaceae
General habit	Herbaceous buns and mats
Origin	Circumpolar/mostly Northern Hemisphere
Garden needs	Sun, cool, regular water

The smaller species tend to require a little more precision and are not considered easy plants. They don't like to dry out in summer but mild winter rains rot them; some go dormant to the point of looking dead during winter. *S. acaulis* (Z1), **top**, is an Arctic-alpine gem, forming a ground-level tight mound, bejewelled with stemless pink, rarely white as pictured, flowers held on dark calyxes. Give it exacting conditions of perfect drainage by planting it high on a crevice edge in a gritty, nutrient-poor soil containing a small amount of clay or humus. Similar treatment is necessary for *S. davidii* (Z3). Like most other silenes, it has larger leaves and inflated flowers with alluring silhouettes. *S. bolanthoides* (Z2) is yet another congested bun-former with large, finely cut, white to light pink flowers. *S. dinarica* (Z4), **bottom**, is another diminutive cushion with lanceolate leaves from the mountains of Romania.

SPIRAEA MORRISONICOLA
MEADOWSWEET

Family	Rosaceae
General habit	Deciduous shrublet
Origin	Taiwanese mountains
Garden needs	Sun, regular water

Recently introduced from the high mountains of Taiwan, the diminutive meadowsweet *Spiraea morrisonicola* (Z5), **left**, gives you your spiraea fix in miniature with a 15 x 30cm (6 x 12in) plant at maturity. Flossy, dark pink flower panicles expand from tight buds above a dome of toothed leaves, which also provide fall color, turning shades of red and yellow. A very classy plant.

Succulents

Crevice gardens offer opportunities for growing succulents outdoors in climates not thought possible. While occasional dry conditions are a classic need for succulents, a surprising number from summer-rain climates will tolerate water, as long as it comes with drainage. Those from higher altitudes can also be surprisingly cold hardy. The following should be tried by any crevice gardener. *Euphorbia clavarioides* (Z6), lion's spore, is endemic to the highlands of South Africa and is a unique succulent which looks like a thornless cactus and grows as a symmetrical dome reaching 15 x 30cm (6 x 12in). Many agaves are native to wild crevices and are stellar in large xeric crevice gardens that offer sufficient winter dryness. Most popular in cold climates are *Agave parryi* var. *couesii* and *A. p.* ssp. *neomexicana* (Z5). Kenton's favorites are the regal *A. utahensis* ssp. *kaibabensis* (Z5) and diminutive mat-forming *A. toumeyana* var. *bella* (Z5). Worth attempting in crevice conditions with rain protection are: *Bergeranthus vespertinus* (syn. *jamesii*) (Z5), *Drosanthemum floribundum* (Z8), *Orostachys spinosa* (Z4), *Ruschia pulvinaris* (Z6), *Sedum spathulifolium* (Z6) and *Stomatium mustellinum* (Z6).

Opposite: *Agave utahensis* ssp. *kaibabensis*
Above: *Euphorbia clavarioides*
Right top: *Sedum spathulifolium*; right middle: *Drosanthemum floribundum*; right bottom: *Bergeranthus vespertinus*

TELESONIX JAMESII

Family	Saxifragaceae
General habit	Dwarf forb
Origin	Colorado Rockies
Garden needs	Shade from hot sun, regular water

The shining star of this two-species genus is *T. jamesii* (Z3), **left**, which grows in rocky, granitic crevices from high in the Colorado Rockies. It looks like a squat heuchera with toothed kidney-shaped leaves and racemes that rise 15cm (6in) high, with well-developed pink saxifrage-like flowers. Its pleasant little clumps are fully herbaceous. It is shy-flowering in cultivation – the secret is to allow its creeping rhizome to become squashed into a tight crevice. Grow it bright and cool.

TEUCRIUM
GERMANDER

Family	Lamiaceae
General habit	Dwarf herbs and shrubs
Origin	Mediterranean
Garden needs	Full sun, dry

Germanders offer toughness of character, charm in form and flower, and versatility in dry, sunny places and poor rocky soil. *T. subspinosum* (Z5), from Majorca, is a stiff and compact sub-shrub reaching 10 x 20cm (4 x 8in) with triangular gray leaves, reddish flowers, and hard twigs forming its own protective cage, which may not be enough to defend it from cats that are mysteriously attracted to it. *T. pyrenaicum* (Z5), **bottom**, from calcareous rock in the Pyrenees, grows twiggy stems at ground level, delivering its fuzzy leaves and two-tone purple and white flowers among the rocks. The contained *T. aroanium* (Z5), **top**, from the Balearic Islands features purple-veined scorpion-like blooms over silver evergreen foliage on a plant only 8cm (3in) high.

TOWNSENDIA
TOWNSEND DAISY

Family	Compositae
General habit	Buns and cushions
Origin	Western North America
Garden needs	Sun, dry

Annuals, biennials, and perennials, desert to alpine, these dwarf plants are coveted by crevice gardeners for their early, often large daisy-like blooms. Most are naturally short-lived and need dry winters. *T. exscapa* (Z3) has large showy white stemless daisies. Kenton's favorite, the most long-lived and early blooming *T. hookeri* (Z3), **top**, has dusty, grassy leaves embedded with gold-hearted white flowers. *T. incana* (Z3), from desert and steppe, is a silver bun. *T. spathulata* is the most petite, with leaf-obscuring dark-eyed flowers. Easy growers include the purple *T. alpigena* (Z3) and very climate-adaptable *T. rothrockii* (Z3). *T. parryi* (Z4), **bottom**, is another great choice for its purple-blue flowers. All are petite ground-huggers.

VERONICA
SPEEDWELL

Family	Plantaginaceae
General habit	Mat-forming perennials
Origin	Temperate Northern Hemisphere
Garden needs	Sunny, dry

Easy dwarf species of *Veronica* have been traditional rock garden plants from the beginning. With flowers in various shades of blue and purple with a characteristic white eye, there is no shortage of species to choose from. Most are flat ground covers but some are small cushions. *V. caespitosa* (Z4), **top**, from high altitudes in Turkey and Lebanon, is one of the smallest of the genus, with gray, hairy leaves and stemless light blue flowers. *V. bombycina* var. *bolkardaghensis* (Z3) from the Taurus Mountains of Turkey is yet another diminutive species of *Veronica* for which drainage is direly needed. An easy creeper for the beginner is the no less beautiful *V. oltensis* (Z3), **bottom**.

ZAUSCHNERIA (NOW EPILOBIUM)
CALIFORNIA FUCHSIA/ FIRE-CHALICE

Family	Onagraceae
General habit	Forbs
Origin	Western North America
Garden needs	Full sun, dry

Possibly the best plant for extending the bloom period in your crevice garden from summer to late fall, as well as a source of vibrant red-oranges for hummingbirds, the zauschies are indispensable for hot, sunny gardens and need some drainage. The genus includes some tall forbs, many of whom are native to crevices, but there exist compact plants with less aggressive rhizomes – even *E. garretii* 'Orange Carpet' (Z4) may be too much for small rock gardens. The best for us are 8–12 cm (3–5in) high, such as the silver-leaved *E. septentrionalis* 'Select Mattole.' (Z7) The fuzzy-leafed 'Everett's Choice' (Z6), **below**, with deep red-orange flowers impresses our mentor ZZ. Seek miniature forms of any species such as the dwarf *E. garretii*, **left**.

Plant lists for specific situations

Easy plants for the novice crevice gardener
- Aethionema subulatum
- Armeria maritima
- Campanula cochlearifolia
- Daphne x rollsdorfii 'Wilhelm Schacht'
- Dianthus erinaceus
- Erigeron compositus
- Globularia cordifolia
- Gypsophila repens 'Rosea'
- Haberlea rhodopensis
- Hormathophylla spinosum 'Roseum'
- Lewisia cotyledon
- Petrophytum caespitosum
- Ramonda myconi
- Saponaria ocymoides 'Rubra Compacta'
- Sempervivum arachnoideum

The choice *Townsendia jonesii var. lutea* in Susan Sims' garden absolutely requires a sunny, dry situation, even in Salt Lake City, Utah.

Daphne x rollsdorfii 'Wilhelm Schacht' is an easy crevice plant.

Challenging plants for the expert crevice gardener
- Campanula raineri
- Castilleja scabrida
- Daphne petraea
- Dionysia aretioides
- Eritrichium nanum
- Iris paradoxa
- Oxalis erythrorhiza
- Paraquilegia anemonoides
- Petunia patagonica
- Saxifraga oppositifolia
- Townsendia aprica (syn. jonesii var. lutea)

Saxifraga oppositifolia is a challenging plant requiring perfect drainage and protection from hot sun, yet whose roots must never be dry.

Plants for dryland crevice gardens
- Acantholimon spp, eg. venustum
- Agave parryi var. couesii
- Anthemis cretica
- Astragalus angustifolius
- Echinocereus spp.
- Erinacea anthyllis
- Eriogonum cespitosum
- Eriogonum kennedyi
- Eriogonum ovalifolium
- Heterotheca jonesii
- Heuchera pulchella
- Lewisia rediviva
- Moltkia petraea
- Penstemon acaulis
- Penstemon crandallii ssp. procumbens
- Penstemon laricifolius
- Phlox hoodii
- Physaria arizonica
- Physaria ovalifolia
- Pterocephalus pinardii
- Salvia caespitosa
- Stenotus acaulis
- Tetraneuris acaulis (syn. Hymenoxys acaulis)
- Teucrium subspinosum
- Townsendia hookeri
- Townsendia spathulata
- Yucca harrimaniae (syn. Y. nana)
- Zauschneria latifolia (syn. Epilobium canum var. latifolium)

Cacti and succulents for crevice gardens

- *Agave parryi*
- *Agave utahensis* ssp. *kaibabensis* (syn. *A. kaibabensis*)
- *Aloinopsis spathulata*
- *Bergeranthus vespertinus* (syn. *B. jamesii*)
- *Coryphantha sulcata*
- *Delosperma congestum*
- *Dudleya cymosa*
- *Echinocereus* spp.
- *Escobaria* spp.
- *Euphorbia clavarioides*
- *Lewisia cotyledon*
- *Maihuenia poeppigii*
- *Opuntia fragilis*
- *Rabiea albipuncta*
- *Ruschia pulvinaris*
- *Sedum spathulifolium*
- *Sempervivum arachnoideum*
- *Sempervivum (Jovibarba) heuffelii*

Cacti and succulents in the garden of John Stireman, Sandy, Utah.

Saxifraga paniculata appreciates moist roots in the summer.

Crevice garden plants for summer-moist climates

- *Azorella trifurcata*
- *Dryas octopetala*
- *Edraianthus pumilio*
- *Gentiana acaulis*
- *Helichrysum sessilioides*
- *Kalmiopsis leachiana*
- *Physoplexis comosa*
- *Rhododendron campylogynum* Myrtilloides Group
- *Saxifraga paniculata*
- *Spiraea morrisonicola*

Lime-loving crevice garden plants

- *Aquilegia jonesii*
- *Asplenium trichomanes*
- *Campanula choruhensis*
- *Convolvulus boissieri*
- *Dianthus erinaceus*
- *Edraianthus pumilio*
- *Erinus alpinus*
- *Globularia incanescens*
- *Gypsophila aretioides*
- *Physoplexis comosa*
- *Polygala calcarea*
- *Potentilla nitida*
- *Saxifraga cebennensis*
- *Paederota bonarota*

Dianthus erinaceus appreciates the higher pH and consequent availability of calcium and magnesium associated with limestone landscapes.

Resources

Public crevice gardens to visit
Allen Centennial Garden, Madison, WI
Alpine Garden Society, Pershore, UK
APEX, Simms St Recreation Center, Arvada, CO
Bangsbo Botanical Garden, Denmark
Bank of the San Juans, Durango, CO
Beacon Hill Park, Victoria, BC, Canada
Betty Ford Alpine Garden, Vail, CO
Botanical Gardens of Silver Springs, Calgary, AB, Canada
Cantigny Park, Wheaton (Chicago), IL
Cheyenne Botanic Gardens, WY
Christchurch Botanical Gardens, New Zealand
Church of St. Jan Nepomucký na Skalka, Prague, Czechia
Colorado Springs Xeriscape Demonstration Garden, CO
Dalhousie Agricultural Campus, NS, Canada
Darts Hill, Surrey, Vancouver, BC, Canada
Denver Botanic Gardens, CO
Denver Botanic Gardens Chatfield Farms, CO
Dunsmuir Botanical Gardens, CA
Durango Botanic Gardens, CO
Explorer's Garden, Pitlochry, Scotland
Far Reaches Farms, Port Townsend, WA
Gardens at Lake Merritt, Oakland, CA
Green Spring Gardens, Alexandria, VA
Heronswood Garden, Kingston, WA
Inniswood Metro Gardens, Columbus, OH
JC Raulston Arboretum, Raleigh, NC
Juniper Level Botanic, Raleigh, NC
Klinta Trädgård, Höör, Sweden
Lissadell House and Gardens, Co. Sligo, Ireland
Memorial University of Newfoundland Botanical Garden, NL, Canada
Missouri Botanical Garden, St Louis, MO
Montreal Botanical Gardens, Quebec, Canada
Montrose Botanical Gardens, CO
Natrona County Extension office, Casper, WY
Nezahat Gökyiğit Botanical Garden, Istanbul
New York Botanical Gardens, NY
Paul J. Ciener Botanical Garden, Kernersville, NC
Royal Botanic Garden Edinburgh, Scotland
RHS Harlow Carr, Harrogate, UK
RHS Wisley, Woking, UK
Rotary Botanical Gardens, Janesville, WI
Smith-Gilbert Gardens, Kennesaw, GA
Strenzfelder Campus Gärten, Bernberg, Germany
SummerHome Garden, Denver, CO
Tilden Regional Park, Berkeley, CA
Tri-River CSU Extension Office, Grand Junction, CO
Tromsø Arctic-Alpine Botanic Garden, Norway
Tübingen Botanischer Garten, Germany
Windsor Community Garden, CO
Yampa River Botanic Park, Steamboat Springs, CO

Resources
Alpine Garden Society (AGS): alpinegardensociety.net
North American Rock Garden Society (NARGS): nargs.org
Pacific Bulb Society: pacificbulbsociety.org
Scottish Rock Garden Club (SRGC): srgc.org.uk
Western Conifer Society: conifersociety.org
Ian Young's Bulb Log: srgc.org.uk/logs
Kenton Seth's blog: kentonjseth.blogspot.com
Panayoti Kelaidis' blog: prairiebreak. blogspot.com
Ontario Rock Garden and Hardy Plant Society's seed germination guide: onrockgarden.com/index.php/germination-guide
Norm Deno Seed germination guide: theseedsite.co.uk/normdeno.html
Cushion plant information: cushionplants.eu
Up-to-date plant names: ipni.org
Rock Garden Plants database: flora.kadel.cz
New Zealand Alpine Garden Society: nzags.com

Seed sources
Alplains, USA: alplains.com
Jelitto, UK: jelitto.com
Mojmír Pavelka, Czechia: pavelkaalpines.cz
Silverhill Seeds, South Africa: silverhillseeds. co.za
Vladimir Staněk, Czechia: e-mail stanekalpines@centrum.cz
Vojtěch Holubec, Czechia: holubec.wbs.cz

Many rock garden societies offer annual seed exchanges.

Specialty nurseries

North America
Arrowhead Alpines: arrowheadalpines.com
Far Reaches Farm: farreachesfarm.com
High Country Gardens; highcountrygardens. com
Plant Delights: plantdelights.com
The Cactus Man: coldhardycactus.com
Wild Ginger Farm: wildgingerfarm.com
Wrightman's Alpines: wrightmanalpines.com

UK
Aberconwy Nursery: aberconwynursery.co.uk
Ashwood Nursery: ashwoodnurseries.com
Border Alpines: borderalpines.co.uk
Kevock Garden Plants: kevockgarden.co.uk
Pottertons Nursery: pottertons.co.uk
Slack Top Alpine Nursery: slacktopnurseries. co.uk

Further reading: books
Bone, Michael, et al. *Steppes: The Plants and Ecology of the World's Semi-Arid Regions*, Portland: Timber Press, 2015
Farrer, Reginald. *My Rock Garden,* London: Edward Arnold, 1911
Farrer, Reginald. (1919) *The English Rock Garden* (Vol 1). Reprint, London: Forgotten Books 2016
Foster, Lincoln. *Rock Gardening: A Guide to Growing Alpines and Other Wildflowers in the American Garden*, New York: Bonanza Books, 1968
Good, John E. G., and Millward, David. *Alpine Plants: Ecology for Gardeners*, Portland: Timber Press, 2007
Grey-Wilson, Christopher. *Cyclamen: A Guide for Gardeners, Horticulturalists and Botanists*, London: Batsford, 1997
Halda, Josef J. *The Genus Gentiana*, Dobré: Sen, 1996
Hills, Laurence. *The Propagation of Alpines*, London: Faber and Faber, 1950
Ingwerson, Will, and Hellyer, Arthur. *Manual of Alpine Plants*, 5th ed., London: Cassell Illustrated, 1994.
Kolaga, Walter A. *All About Rock Gardens and Plants,* New York: Doubleday, 1966
Korn, Peter. *Peter Korn's Garden: Giving Plants What They Want*, Peter Korn, 2013
Mineo, Baldassare. *Rock Garden Plants: A Color Encyclopedia*, Portland: Timber Press, 1999
McGregor, Malcolm. *Saxifrages: A Definitive Guide to the 2000 Species, Hybrids and Cultivars*, Portland: Timber Press, 2008
Nold, Robert. *High and Dry: Gardening with Cold-Hardy Dryland Plants*, Portland: Timber Press, 2008
Nold, Robert. *Penstemons*, Portland: Timber Press, 1999
Ogden, Scott and Springer Ogden, Lauren. *Plant-driven Design: Creating Gardens That Honor Plants, Place, and Spirit*, Portland: Timber Press, 2008
Pojar, Jim, and MacKinnon, Andy. *Alpine Plants of British Columbia, Alberta, and Northwest North America*, Edmonton: Lone Pine Publishing, 2013
Robinson, William. *Alpine Flowers for English Gardens*, London: John Murray, 1870
Symons-Jeune, B. H. B. *Natural Rock Gardening*, 3rd ed., London: Country Life, 1955
Thomas, Graham Stuart. *The Rock Garden and Its Plants: From Grotto to Alpine House*, Portland: Timber Press, 1989
White, Robin. Daphnes: *A Practical Guide for Gardeners*, Portland: Timber Press, 2006
Zvolánek. Zdenčk. *The Crevice Garden and its Plants*, AGS Publications Ltd, 2006

Further reading: articles
CMG GardenNotes #214, *Estimating Soil Texture*, December 2015. https://cmg.extension.colostate.edu/Gardennotes/214.pdf
Elliot, Brent. 'The British Rock Garden in the Twentieth Century', *Occasional Papers from the RHS Lindley Library*, V6, May 2011
Ferguson, Stephanie. 'Sun, Stone, and Water', *Rock Garden Quarterly*, Vol 69 #3, Summer 2011 56. Schematic Drawings by David Ferguson, North American Rock Garden Society, Part 1, Page 210: https://www.nargs.org/sites/default/files/free-rgq-downloads/VOL_69_NO_3_0.pdf. Part 2: Fall 2011, Vol 69 #4 Page 314 https://www.nargs.org/sites/default/files/free-rgq-downloads/VOL_69_NO_4_1.pdf
Johnston, B. C. *Armeria maritima ssp. sibirica: a technical conservation assessment*, USDA Forest Service, Rocky Mountain Region, 2007, p8
Vydra, Otakar. 'In Czechoslovakia', *Rocky Mountain Alpines*, American Rock Garden Society Publications Committee, 294–300. Portland: Timber Press, 1986

Index

Page numbers in *italic* type refer to illustrations or their captions; **bold** numbers refer to plant profiles.

Photo Credits

223

The public crevice garden
at Silver Springs, Calgary.

Kenton J. Seth ❯

Kenton J. Seth is a Colorado-based garden designer who gets his hands dirty from his hometown to gardens abroad, specializing in crevice gardens, xeric natives, and meadows. Kenton worked in public horticulture at a local botanic garden for ten years and then in the nursery trade for several more before starting his design/build company, Paintbrush Gardens, in 2013. His projects are fortified by wild-hunting seed and growing plants in his small nursery. He writes for a variety of local, national and international magazines and travels to lecture, from across town to across the seas. He is a member of the Colorado Native Plant Society, various plant-specific clubs, the Scottish Rock Garden Club, the Alpine Garden Society and is most active in the Rocky Mountain Chapter of the North American Rock Garden Society. He and his partner Tori grow vegetables, ride bikes and watch sunsets over the canyon country in Fruita, Colorado.

Paul Spriggs ❯

Paul Spriggs has been rock gardening for 23 years and building crevice gardens for the last 16. He is a professional gardener and landscaper, and an avid plant explorer, photographer and mountaineer. He has a passion for all wild plants, especially miniatures, collecting and cultivating them in various gardens in his hometown of Victoria, British Columbia. Paul learned the art of crevice garden from one of its innovators, Zdeněk Zvolánek. He has built many crevice gardens in public parks and private homes ranging from small feature troughs to large installations with many tons of stone. Paul is passionate about spreading the crevice gospel through lectures and workshops, by having served as president of the Vancouver Island Rock and Alpine Garden Society, and by proselytizing to whomever will listen. Paul can be caught growing sunflowers and dahlias as a guilty pleasure and hanging out with his growing family.